300 最常用的汉字

300 Most Commonly Used Chinese Characters

Preface

Recently, artificial intelligence (commonly known as AI) has taken the world by storm. People are astonished to discover that AI has mastered human languages and can communicate effortlessly with us.

How did AI learn human languages? Through statistics. AI has analyzed an enormous amount of data from books, articles, and social media, using statistical methods to identify patterns within human language. One approach involves examining the frequency of word usage and predicting the most likely word to follow in a given sequence.

This makes me wonder: can humans learn a language by borrowing this strategy from AI? For example, in Chinese, we know the average frequency of each word's usage. What if we focus on learning the most frequently used words first?

This strategy has not yet been thoroughly tested. There are several reasons why teachers have not adopted this approach. First, students—especially young ones—are often more interested in learning words like animal names. Second, pronunciation is typically introduced early on, so words are chosen to cover a broad range of sounds. Then, of course, there is grammar.

For older students, however, learning the most frequently used words first may prove to be more efficient. This book is designed to help learners quickly gain the ability to read in Chinese.

We selected the first 300 most commonly used characters. In a typical Chinese article, this group of charaters accounts for about 67.7% of the text—roughly two out of every three characters. Since people are generally good at guessing unknown words while reading, knowing the first 300 characters could enable learners to start reading in Chinese. By continuing to read in Chinese, learners can rapidly expand their vocabulary and improve their language skills.

At the end of the book, we've included an additional list of 300 characters. These characters are commonly used in conjunction with the first 300 to form phrases. Together, all 600 charaters cover approximately 80% of the charaters in a text.

For each word, we don't attempt to explain every possible meaning. These words are frequently used because they form parts of numerous phrases. We focus on explaining the root meaning first, followed by their most common uses. Readers are encouraged to use their imagination since many phrases derive their meanings from the roots of the words. For example, the phrase 马上 is formed by the words 马 (horse) and 上 (up). 马 means "horse," and 上 means "up." What does 马上 mean? On the surface, it means "on the horse." What does it imply when you're on the horse? You're ready to go. Yes, that's exactly the meaning—马上 means "immediately."

If you decide to study Chinese by learning the most frequently used words first, we'd love to hear about your experience. Please leave your feedback in this book's review section. Your comments will not only help others decide where to focus their efforts but also assist us in improving the book.

Finally,

祝你马到成功!

The four central characters in this phrase are among the first 300 characters: 你 — "you" 马 — "horse" 到 — "arrive" 成 — "complete"

You get the idea!

1 的 de

表示修饰、所属或属性

我的 书
红色的 苹果
手机 是 你的？ 是（我）的。

Of

Indicates modification, belonging or attribute

My book
Red apple
Is the phone yours? It is (mine).

2 一 yī

表示数量和顺序

一个 人
第一 名
一生 一世 只有 一次。
词组：一起、一定、一路

One

Indicates quantity and order

A person
First place
One lifetime, only once.
Phrase: together, definitely, all the way

3 了 liǎo

表示完成或变化

下雨了。
他 来了。
词组：了解、了不起

End

Indicates completion or change

It's raining.
He's coming.
Phrase: understand, amazing

4 是 shì

表示肯定

他 是 老师。
会议 是 三点 开始的。
词组：是非、是否

Be

To express affirmation

He is a teacher.
The meeting starts at three o'clock.
Phrases: right and wrong, whether

5 不 bù

表示否定

他 不 喜欢 喝 咖啡。
你 是不是 学生?
词组：不会、不用、不行

Not

Expresses negation

He doesn't like coffee.
Are you a student (or not)?
Phrase: no (not capable), no (not necessary), no (not allowed)

6 我 wǒ

说话者自身

我 爱 你。
他 帮助了 我。
我的 朋友 住在 北京。
词组：我们

I, me

Speaker himself

I love you.
He helped me.
My friend lives in Beijing.
Phrase: We

7 在 zài

表示存在、时间、地点

妈妈 在家吗?
我 正在 写 作业。
在 飞机上
词组：现在、存在、所在

In, at

Indicates existence, time, and place

Is mom home?
I am doing my homework.
On the plane
Phrase: now, existence, where something is

8 人 rén

人类、个人

街上 有 很多人。
为 人民 服务。
她 是 好人。
词组：人群、人们、商人、人生

Human

Human, individual

There are many people on the street.
Serve the people.
She is a good person.
Phrases: crowd, people, businessman, life

9 有 yǒu

表示拥有、所属、存在

王 先生 有 很多 朋友。
桌子 上 有 一杯 水。
昨天 有 一场 比赛。
词组：有时、有关、有可能

Have

Indicates possession, belonging, existence

Mr. Wang has many friends.
There is a glass of water on the table.
There was a game yesterday.
Phrases: sometimes, about, possibly

10 这 zhè

指代近处或当前

这是 什么?
这本书 很 有趣。
这 几天 很忙。
词组：这里、这些、这样

This

Refers to the near or present

What is this?
This book is interesting.
I have been very busy these days.
Phrase: here, these, this way

11 他 tā

指代男性或泛指第三人

他 每天 跑步。
如果 有人 找我，请 让他 稍 等。
他们 在 相爱。
词组：其他、他人

He, him

Refers to a male or a third person in general

He runs every day.
If someone comes to see me, please ask him to wait.
They are in love.
Phrases: other, someone else

12 来 lái

表示移动、方向、意愿

春天 来了。
请 来 办公室 一趟。
让 我 来。
词组：以来、起来、来年

Come

Indicates movement, direction, willingness

Spring is coming.
Please come to the office.
Let me do it.
Phrases: since, up, next year

13 个 gè
计量个体单位

Individual unit of measurement

一个 房间 住 两个 人。
每个 人 都要 努力。
这个 想法 不错。
词组：这个、那个、整个、个别

Two people live in one room.
Everyone has to work hard.
This is a good idea.
Phrases: this, that, the whole, individual

14 你 nǐ

You

对话的对方

The other party in the conversation

你好！
谢谢 你。
你们 公司 有 多少 人？

Hello!
Thank you.
How many people are there in your company?

15 说 shuì

Say, explain

言语表达

Verbal expression

妈妈 说 要 早点 回家。
她 说 英语 很 流利。
天气 预报 说 今天 要 下雨。
词组：说话、说明、说笑

Mom said she would go home early.
She speaks English fluently.
The weather forecast says it will rain today.
Phrases: speak, explain, joke

16 上 shàng

Up

表示位置高或靠前

A high position or close to the front

桌子 上 有 一本 书。
上 有 天，下 有 地。
好好 学习，天天 向上。
词组：上午、上学、上车

There is a book on the table.
There is heaven above and earth below.
Study hard and make progress every day.
Phrase: morning, go to school, get in the car

17 到 dào

Arrive

到达或完成

To arrive or complete

我 到 上海 了。
会议 到 明天 结束。
到 目前 为止，一切 顺利。
词组：到达、看到、遇到

I have arrived in Shanghai.
The meeting ends tomorrow.
So far, so good.
Phrases: to arrive, to see, to meet

18 就 jiù

At once

强调时间、条件或程度

Emphasize time, conditions or degree

我 就走，马上 回来。
下雨 就 不 出去 了。
如果 累了，就 休息 一下。
词组：就是、早就、就近

I will leave now and come back soon.
I will not go out if it rains.
If you are tired, take a rest right away.
Phrase: just, long ago, near

19 着 zhe

表示动作或状态的持续

Indicates the continuation of an action or state

她 笑着 说："门 开着。"
墙上 挂着 一幅 画。
我 等着 你。
词组：朝着、沿着、跟着

She smiled and said, "The door is open."
There is a painting hanging on the wall.
I'll be waiting for you.
Phrase: twoards, along, follow

20 大 dà

Big

表示数量多或位置靠前

Indicates a large number or a front position

小河 流入 大海。
大姐 有 一个 小孩。
要 做 大事，不要 做 大官。
词组：大学、大约、伟大

A small river flows into the sea.
The eldest sister has a child.
To do great things, not to be a high official.
Phrase: university, about, great

21 们 mén
表示人的复数

Indicates the plural form of people

我们 是 一家 人。
你们 好。
朋友们 今日 相聚。
词组：我们、你们、他们、她们

We are a family.
Hello you guys.
Friends gather today.
Phrase: we, you, they, they (women)

22 道 dào
表示路径、方法或规律

Way
Indicates a path, method or law

道路 畅通 无阻。
这条 街道 禁止 通行。
道家 认为 "道" 是 宇宙 万物 的 本源。
词组：知道、道理、道德、道谢

The road is unobstructed.
This street is closed to traffic.
Taoists believe that "Tao" is the origin of all things in the universe.
Phrases: know, reason, morality, thank you

23 那 nà
指代远处

That
Refers to something distant

那 座 山 很高。
那 时候 我 还小。
我 来自 纽约，那里 还有 爸爸 妈妈。
词组：那样、那么、那些

That mountain is very high.
I was still a kid at that time.
I am from New York, where my parents still are.
Phrases: that kind, so, those

24 么 me
后缀或语气助词

Suffix or modal particle

这 是 什么?
多么 美 的 风景!
为什么 不 告诉 我?
词组：这么、那么、怎么样

What is this?
What a beautiful view!
Why didn't you tell me?
Phrase: so, so, how

25 也 yě — Also

表示类同、补充或强调语气

她 聪明，也 很 努力。
他 去，我 也 去。
我 什么也 不 知道。
词组：也许、也好、也就是说

To express similarity, complement or emphasis

She is not just smart but also hardworking.
If he goes, I will go too.
I don't know anything.
Phrase: maybe, all right, that is to say

26 地 (1) dì (2) de — Earth[1]

（1）土地（2）表示动作的方式、状态或程度

地[1]球 是 圆的。
他 头也不回 地[2] 走了。
雨 不停地[2] 下。

(1) Land (2) Indicates the manner, state or degree of an action

The earth is round.
He left without looking back.
The rain kept falling.

27 子 zi — Child

子女、词的后缀

他家 儿子 是个 独生子。
鬼子*不会 用 筷子。
孔子 是个 教育家。
词组：子公司、桌子、胖子
*鬼子曾是对外国人的侮辱性称呼，如今在大多数情况下是昵称。

Children, suffix of a word

His son is an only child.
Son of a ghost* can't use chopsticks.
Confucius is an educator.
Phrases: subsidiary, table, fat man
*Son of a ghost was once an insulting name for foreigners, but now it is a nickname in most cases.

28 下 xià — Down

表示位置低或靠后

下雨了，楼下 到处 是 水。
下班后，他 喜欢 下 围棋。
别急 下 结论。
词组：下级、下午、下飞机

Indicates a low or backward position

It's raining, and there's water everywhere downstairs.
After get off work, he likes to play Go.
Don't jump to conclusions.
Phrase: subordinate, afternoon, get off the plane

29 出 chū

表示从内到外、由近到远

出门 在外，多 交朋友。
太阳 出来了吗?
别 出 声音。
词组：出事、出口、出众

Out

Indicates from inside to outside, from near to far
When you are traveling, make more friends.
Is the sun out?
Don't make any noise.
Phrase: accident, exit/export, outstanding

30 时 shí

时间

一 小时 六十 分钟。
按时 吃饭 有利 健康。
机 不可 失，时 不再来。
词组：有时、及时、时代

Time

Time

One hour has sixty minutes.
Eating on time is good for your health.
Opportunity is fleeting, time never comes back.
Phrases: sometimes, timely, era

31 看 kàn

用眼睛观察

你 看见 那个 看手机的 人吗?
有空 来 看我。
是不是 郊游 要看 天气。
词组：看护、好看、看法、看得起

Look

Observe with your eyes

Do you see the person looking at the phone?
Come and see me when you have time.
Whether we can go on an outing depends on the weather.
Phrases: care, good-looking, opinion, respect

32 要 yào

索取、希望得到

孩子 要 糖 吃。
你 要 小心。
会议 要 开始了。
词组：要点、要求、重要、简要

Want

To ask for, to hope for

The child wants candy.
You should be careful.
The meeting is about to begin.
Phrase: key points, requirements, important, brief

33 她 tā

女性第三人称

第一次 见到 她 时，她 还是 一个 学生。
爱 她 就要 爱 她的 一切。
她 和 他 是 天生 一对。
词组：她们

She, her

Female third person

When I first met her, she was still a student.
To love her is to love everything about her.
She and he are a perfect match.
Phrase: They

34 中 zhōng

指方位、范围或状态

中心 有 一张 桌子。
工作 中 的 问题 要 及时 解决。
"中国" 一词 最早 出现 在 3000 多年 前。
词组：家中、中等、中奖

Center

Refers to position, range or state

There is a table in the center.
Problems at work should be solved in a timely manner.
The word "China" first appeared more than 3,000 years ago.
Phrase: home, middle, winning

35 没 méi

否定存在、动作或状态

没有 人 感 兴趣。
钱包 没丢。
他 还 没 吃饭。
词组：没事、没关系、没心没肺

Not

Negation of existence, action or state

No one is interested.
The wallet is not lost.
He hasn't eaten yet.
Phrase: It's okay, it doesn't matter, heartless

36 然 rán

对、如此、词尾表示状态

我 说了 我的 看法，他 听后 不以为然。
人 必然 会 死亡。
然后 呢?
词组：自然、突然、偶然

Yes, so, the ending of the word indicates a state

I told him my opinion, but he didn't agree with it.
People will inevitably die.
And then?
Phrase: natural, sudden, accidental

37 里 lǐ — Inside

内部方位、长度单位

Internal position, unit of length

老师 在 教室 里。
1 里 等于 500 米，一 公里 等于 1000 米。
他 心里 高兴。
词组：乡里、表里

The teacher is in the classroom.
1 li is equal to 500 meters, and 1 kilometer is equal to 1000 meters.
He is happy.
Phrases: township, inside and outside

38 为 wéi — For

作为，表示目的和对象、

To act, express purpose and object,

为官 当 为民 请命。
一 分 为 二。
为 天下 笑。
词组：为何、行为、认为

As an official one should plead for the people.
One divided becomes two.
Laughed by the whole world.
Phrase: why, behavior, think

39 过 guò — Pass

经过

Pass by

穿过 马路 就 到了。
过年了，你 回家吗?
他 当过 商人。
词组：过去、过分、过期、过敏

Just cross the road and you will arrive.
It is the New Year, are you going home?
He used to be a businessman.
Phrases: past, excessive, expired, allergy

40 自 zì — Self

自身、起点

Self, starting point

我 相信 我 自己。
长江 和 黄河 都 自西 向东 流。
自 一月 一日 起，公司 放 三 天 假。
词组：自由、自学、自然

I believe in myself.
The Long River and the Yellow River both flow from west to east.
From January 1st, the company will have three days off.
Phrase: freedom, self-study, nature

41 好 (1) hǎo (2) hào

(1) 正向评价 (2) 喜爱

好¹人有好¹报。
病好¹了心情也好¹了。
小王 爱好²旅游。
词组：友好¹、美好¹、好²奇

Good

(1) Positive evaluation (2) Like

Good people are rewarded.
The illness is cured and the mood is better.
Xiao Wang likes traveling.
Phrase: friendly, beautiful, curious

42 得 (1) dé (2) de

(1) 获得 (2) 表结果或程度

他得¹奖了，很得¹意。
得¹人心者，得¹天下。
我拿得²动。
词组：得¹失、心得¹、不得¹

Get[1]

(1) To obtain (2) To indicate a result or degree

He won a prize and was very pleased.
He who wins the hearts of the people wins the world.
I can handle it.
Phrase: gain and loss, lessons learned, not allowed

43 去 qù

空间和时间上的离开

去广州出差。
放假了，人去楼空。
去年冬天不冷。
词组：上去、去处、过去

Go

Departure in space or time

Going on a business trip to Guangzhou.
It's vacation time, people leave and the building is empty.
Last winter was not cold.
Phrase: go up, destination, past

44 可 kě

肯定、加强语气

没有政府的许可，公司是不可能开张的。
可口可乐很可口。
这菜可好吃了。
词组：认可、可以、可悲

Can

Affirmation, strengthening tone

Without government permission, the company cannot open.
Coca-Cola is delicious.
This dish is really delicious.
Phrase: approve, allow, sad

45 会 huì

Meet

聚合、能够

Gather, to be able to

奥委会 正在 开会。
我 会 英语 和 中文。
宴会 晚上 八点 开始。
词组：会面、委员会、会议室

The Olympic Committee is meeting.
I can speak English and Chinese.
The banquet starts at 8pm.
Phrases: meet face to face, committee,
meeting room

46 天 tiān

Sky

自然和抽象的天空

Natural and abstract sky

鸟 在 天空 飞。
三天 后 天 会 晴。
天 知道!
词组：天地、天才、天堂

Birds are flying in the sky.
The sky will be clear in three days.
God knows!
Phrase: heaven and earth, genius, heaven

47 还 (1) huán (2) hái

Return[1]

(1) 返回 (2) 表示延续

(1) Return (2) Indicates continuation

图书馆 的 书 你 还[1] 了 吗?
别人 打 他，他 也 不 还[1] 手。
今天 比 昨天 还[2] 冷 。
词组：还[1] 乡、还[1] 击、归还[1]

Have you returned the books from the
library?
He didn't fight back when someone hit
him.
It's colder today than yesterday.
Phrase: back to hometown, fight back,
return items

48 心 xīn

Heart

生理与抽象的心

Physiological and abstract heart

我的 心跳 很快。
人 有 心情 好的 时候，也有
伤心的 时候。
关心 别人，也要 关心 自己。
词组：爱心、中心、心思

My heart beats very fast.
People have good days and sad days.
Caring for others, also caring for
yourself.
Phrase: love, center, thought

49 后 hòu

时间或空间次序、皇后

Back, queen

Order of time or space, Queen

请走 后门。
前人 栽树，后人 乘凉。
后天 是 儿童 节。
词组：后面、后辈、后悔

Please go through the back door.
Those who came before plant trees,
those who come after enjoy the shade.
The day after tomorrow is Children's
Day.
Phrases: behind, younger generation,
regret

50 以 yǐ

使用、凭借

With

Use, rely on

辩论 要 以理 服人。
他 以为 自己 已经 赢了。
物 以 稀 为 贵。
词组：以及、以前、可以

In a debate, one must convince others
with reason.
He thought he had already won.
Scarcity makes things valuable.
Phrases: and, before, can

51 小 xiǎo

描述事物微小、次要；谦称和
昵称

Small

Describes something as small or minor;
humble and nickname

一千 不是 一个 小 数目。
好 可爱 的 小猫。
小林 开了 一个 小店。
词组：小孩、小弟、小人

One thousand is not a small amount.
Such a cute kitten.
Xiao Lin opened a small shop.
Phrases: child, younger brother, villain

52 都 (1) dū (2) dōu

(1)中心城市 (2)全部、表示强
调

Capital, all

(1) Central city (2) All, to emphasize

京都[1] 曾经 是[1] 日本的 首都[1]。
每 一个 人 都[2] 很 重要。
他 忙得 连 饭 都[2] 没吃。
词组：首都[1]、都[1]市、都[2]是

Kyoto was once the capital of Japan.
Everyone is important.
He was so busy that he didn't even have
a meal.
Phrases: capital, city, all

53 和 hé — Peace, and

表示融洽、联合

Indicates harmony and union

我 和 他 相处 很 和睦。
3 加 2 的 和 是 5。
今天 天气 很 温和。
词组：和平、和气、和棋

He and I get along very well.
The sum of 3 plus 2 is 5.
The weather is very mild today.
Phrases: peace, harmony, draw

54 对 duì — Right

正确、对应

Correct, corresponding

答案 是 对的，方法 不对。
我 是 对事 不 对人。
我 买了 一对 耳环。
词组：对待、对门、对称

The answer is right, but the method is wrong.
I am focusing on the issue, not the person.
I bought a pair of earrings.
Phrase: treat, across the door, symmetrical

55 想 xiǎng — Think

思维活动、内心感受

Thinking activities, inner feelings

你 想想 办法。
我 想 他 今天 不会 来了。
这个 想法 有点 想象力。
词组：思想、理想、想必

You think of a way.
I don't think he will come today.
This idea is a bit imaginative.
Phrases: thought, ideal, presumably

56 能 néng — Can, energy

表示能力、能量、许可

Indicates ability, energy, permission

他 能 开车。
能量 是 守恒的。
飞机 可能 晚点 了。
词组：才能、功能、太阳能

He can drive.
Energy is conserved.
The plane may be delayed.
Phrase: talent, function, solar energy

57 起 qǐ — Rise

表示开始、上升
Indicates starting, rising

起床后的第一句话是"早晨好。"
The first thing you say after getting up is "Good morning."

起点在前面。
The starting point is in front.

飞机起飞了。
The plane took off.

词组：起源、想起、起跑
Phrase: origin, remember, start

58 之 zhī — Of

相当于的或他/她/它
Equivalent to of or he/she/it

长生不老是求之不得的。
Immortality is something that is highly desired but impossible to obtain.

消息传来，人人为之鼓舞。
When the news came, everyone was encouraged (because of it).

如有冒犯之处，请原谅。
Please forgive me if it is offensive.

词组：之间、之后、之一
Phrases: between, after, one of

59 手 shǒu — Hand

身体部位、引申为技能
Body part, extended to skill

手心手背都是肉。
The palm and back of the hand are all flesh.

水手在船上工作。
The sailor works on the ship.

他俩握手言和了。
They shook hands and made peace.

词组：手法、手枪、能手
Phrases: technique, pistol, expert

60 而 ér

连词
Conjunctions

花不仅漂亮，而且香。
Flowers are not only beautiful, but also fragrant.

人不能言而无信。
People should not break their promises.

你为什么而工作?
Why do you work?

词组：而已、而今、而是
Phrases: only, now, but

61 只 (1)zhī (2)zhǐ — One, only

(1)单数单位 (2)限定程度   (1) singular unit (2) limited level

一只¹鸡，二 会 飞，三个 铜板 买来的。
只²要 好吃 我 就 喜欢。
我 只²爱 一人。
词组：只²是、只²许、只¹身

One chicken, two can fly, three copper coins I bought.
As long as it tastes good, I like it.
I only love one person.
Phrase: only, only allow, alone

62 生 shēng — Living

与生命、生长、存在相关   Related to life, growth, and existence

人 一 出生，就 注定 要 死 。
祝 你 生日 快乐!
人生 不管 发生 什么，都是 一种 精彩。
词组：生活、生病、生锈

When a person is born, he is destined to die.
Happy birthday to you!
No matter what happens in life, it is wonderful.
Phrases: life, illness, rust

63 什 shén — What

疑问代词、感叹   Interrogative pronouns, exclamations

你 想 说 什么?
他 好像 知道 些 什么。
什么! 他 竟然 赢了?
词组：为什么、没什么

What do you want to say?
He seems to know something.
What! He actually won?
Phrases: why, nothing

64 身 shēn — Body

躯体，引申为自我、地位、生命   Body, extended to self, status, life

身高 1 米 82。
我 身份证 丢了。
终身 大事 不可 轻易。
词组：自身、出身、一身

Height 1.82 meters.
I lost my ID card.
Don't take life events lightly.
Phrases: self, origin, one's whole life

65 头 tóu　Head

头部，引申为起点、顶端、首领

Head, extended to starting point, top, leader

她 摇头 说不。
She shook her head and said no.

头头们 都在 会议室。
The leaders are all in the meeting room.

电影 开头 不错。
The movie has a good begining.

词组：里头、头发、盼头
Phrase: inside, hair, hope

66 样 yàng　Shape

指事物的形状、种类
Refers to the shape or type of things

全球 变暖 正 悄悄 改变 地球 的 模样。
Global warming is quietly changing the appearance of the earth.

这个 样式 还 可以。
This style is OK.

给 他们 几个 样品。
Give them a few samples.

词组：花样、多样、榜样
Phrase: trick, variety, example

67 事 shì　Thing

指人类活动、事件、职业
Refers to human activities, events, and occupations

没事了，可以下班了。
It's done, you can get off work.

光 着急 也 不是 事儿 。
It's no good just to be anxious.

路上 有 两个 事故。
There were two accidents on the road.

词组：事件、故事、从事
Phrases: event, story, engaged in

68 多 duō　Many

表示量大、程度高或超出
Indicates large quantity, high degree or exceeding

多谢。
Thank you very much.

今年 秋天 多雨。
It rained a lot this autumn.

你 多大了？
How old are you?

词组：多少、多心、好多
Phrase: how much, suspicious, a lot

69 己 jǐ — Self

指代自身、个人

Refers to oneself, an individual

我 喜欢 自己 现在 的 样子。
不 以 物 喜，不 以 己 悲。
己 所 不 欲，勿 施 于 人 。
词组：利己、知己、己任

I like the way I am now.
Do not let material joys elate you, nor personal setbacks depress you.
What you don't desire for yourself, do not inflict upon others。
Phrases: self-interest, a confidant, responsibility

70 家 jiā — Home

指住所、血缘、归属

Refers to residence, blood relationship, belonging

我 老家 四川。
病人 的 家属 可以 探访 。
教授 是 法学 专家。
词组：家庭、国家、成家

My hometown is Sichuan.
The patient's family members can visit.
The professor is a legal expert.
Phrases: family, country, get married

71 面 miàn — Face

指人脸、物体的表层或朝向

Refers to face，the surface of an object or direction

他的 面孔 好 熟悉。
面朝 大海，春暖 花开。
纸的 正面 反面 都 写着 字。
词组：平面、表面、面条

His face is so familiar.
Facing the sea, spring is in full bloom.
There are words written on both sides of the paper.
Phrase: plane, surface, noodle

72 知 zhī — Know

认知、了解、与智慧相关

Cognition, understanding, related to wisdom

我 知道了。
学习 科学 知识 不 容易。
小梅 知情 达理。
词组：知觉、良知、知音

I know.
It is not easy to learn scientific knowledge.
Xiao Mei is sensible and considerate.
Phrase: perception, conscience, soulmate

73 开 kāi — Open

表示开启、扩展或解除封闭状态

Indicates opening, expanding or unblocking a closed state

把 房间 灯 打开 ，马上 开会。
花开 花落 是 自然 现象。
一场 激战 即将 开始。
词组：开发、开张、开车

Turn on the lights in the room and hold the meeting immediately.
Flowers blooming and falling is a natural phenomenon.
A fierce battle is about to begin.
Phrase: develop, business open, drive

74 如 rú — As if

相似、遵循、假设或列举

Similar, follow, assume or list

细雨，如烟，如雾。
如果 想 成功，就 得 努力。
祝 你 事事 如愿！
词组：如一、假如、例如

Drizzle, like smoke, like fog.
If you want to succeed, you have to work hard.
May everything go as you wish!
Phrase: remaining the same, if, for example

75 无 wú — No

表示不存在、否定或虚空

Indicates non-existence, negation or emptiness

我 是 身无 分文。
爱情 是 无价的。
这件 事 无法 办到。
词组：无限、无需、虚无

I am penniless.
Love is priceless.
This thing cannot be done.
Phrases: infinite, unnecessary, nothingness

76 现 xiàn — Appear, now

指显露、当下

Refers to reveal, present

大 明星 还没有 现身?
现在 没人 用 现金。
对于 现代 艺术 我 一点 不懂。
词组：现实、现场、表现

The big star hasn't shown up yet?
No one uses cash now.
I don't understand anything about modern art.
Phrases: reality, scene, performance

77 很 hěn — Very

表示程度高、状态的强化

Indicates a high degree or an enhanced state

我 很 喜欢 篮球。
I like basketball very much.

干得 很好，很 漂亮!
You did a great job!

很多 人 都 去 看 足球 了。
Many people went to watch soccer.

词组：很久、很可能、很快
Phrase: a long time, very likely, very soon

78 点 diǎn — Dot, tiny

微小痕迹、少量或时间单位

A tiny trace, a small amount, or a unit of time

雨点儿 落在 水面 上。
The raindrops fell on the water.

我们 可以 在 那儿 种 一点儿 花。
We can plant a few flowers there.

列车 三点钟 到站。
The train arrives at three o'clock.

词组：小数点、指点、点心
Phrase: decimal point, give advice, dessert

79 前 qián — In front

表示方位靠前、时间早，或推进

Indicates being ahead, early, or advancing

前面的 路 还 很长 很长。
The road ahead is still very long.

注意 前方 有人 骑车。
Be careful, there are people riding bicycles ahead.

前任 辞职 了。
The predecessor resigned.

词组：前天、前提、提前
Phrase: the day before yesterday, premise, in advance

80 发 fā — Dispatch, hair

送出、出现、毛发
Send out, appear, hair

火箭 发射 成功。
The rocket was launched successfully.

产品 开发 很 顺利。
Product development went smoothly.

头发 长了，该 理发 了。
The hair has grown long, it's time to get a haircut.

词组：发现、发表、发病
Phrase: discover, publish, get sick

81 经 jīng

Pass through

织布的纵线、经过、管理、权威
经纬度 是 经度 与 纬度 组成的 坐标 系统。
1 路车 经过 天安门。
经济 不好，经理 再好 也 没用。
词组：经常、经典、经纪

The longitudinal line of weaving, passing, management, authority
Longitude and latitude are coordinate systems composed of longitude and latitude.
Bus No. 1 passes Tiananmen Square.
If the economy is bad, no matter how good the manager is, it will be useless.
Phrases: often, classic, agent

82 情 qíng

Emotion

人类情感、事物状态

Human emotions, state of things

人是有情感的动物。
他有点不顺利，情绪不好。
真实情况还好。
词组：感情、爱情、情侣

Humans are emotional animals.
He is not doing well and is in a bad mood.
The real situation is not bad.
Phrase: emotion, love, couple

83 把 bǎ

Hold

手持、用于强调

Hold, used to emphasize

开车 要 把握 好 方向盘。
把门关上。
你能把他怎么样？
词组：把持、一把、把门

Hold the steering wheel well when driving.
Close the door.
What can you do to him?
Phrases: hold, handful, guard the door

84 老 lǎo

Old

年老、久远、尊敬、亲昵

Old, long-time, respectful, intimate

老了，头发白了。
这本书老少皆宜。
大家现在喊老张张老。
词组：老公、老师、老花

Old now, with gray hair.
This book is suitable for all ages.
Now everyone calls Lao Zhang Zhang Lao (authoritative expert).
Phrases: husband, teacher, presbyopia

85 些 xiē

Some

少量、不确指的量

A small amount, an indefinite amount

买些 水 回来。
你 还 需要 些 什么?
这些 是 给你的。
词组: 一些、有些、好些

Buy some water on your way back.
What else do you need?
These are for you.
Phrase: some, some, better

86 话 huà

Talk

言语

Speech

看来 你 心中 有 话 要说。
今天 的 话题 是 人工 智能。
给 客户 打个 电话。
词组: 说话、话剧、笑话

It seems that you have something to say.
Today's topic is artificial intelligence.
Make a phone call to the client.
Phrases: speech, drama, joke

87 已 yǐ

Already

停止、表示过去和完成

Stop, indicate past and completion

飞机 已经 起飞 了。
死 而后 已。
事 已 至此, 不用 再 说了。
词组: 以往、已故、不得已

The plane has taken off.
Cease only with death.
It is over now, no need to talk about it anymore.
Phrase: in the past, deceased, had to

88 又 yòu

Again

表重复或继续、加强语气

Indicates repetition or continuation, strengthens the tone

他 又 迟到 了 。
天气 又冷 又 多风 。
你 又 不是 小孩!
词组: 又说又笑、又名

He is late again.
The weather is cold and windy.
You are not a child!
Phrase: talking and laughing, also known as

89 声 shēng Sound

物理声音、语言表达、名誉

Physical sound, verbal expression, reputation

声音 太 大了。
The sound is too loud.

我 多次 声明过 此事 与 我们 无关。
I have stated many times that this matter has nothing to do with us.

品牌 是 公司 多年来 积累的 声誉。
Brand is the reputation accumulated by the company over the years.

词组：掌声、雷声、声势
Phrase: applause, thunder, momentum

90 意 yì Thought

未说出口的思维、意图、情感

Unspoken thoughts, intentions, and emotions

每个人 都把 自己的 意见 说一下。
Everyone please express your opinions.

小李 有情 有义。
Xiao Li is loyal and compassionate.

有点 意思。
It's a bit interesting.

词组：意义、意外、诗意
Phrases: meaning, surprise, poetic charm

91 于 yú In, on, at

表时间、地点、对象等关系

Indicates the relationship between time, place, object, etc.

李敏 生于 72 年 2 月 22 日。
Li Min was born on February 22, 72.

霜叶 红于 二月 花。
Frost-touched leaves are redder than the blossoms of February.

成功 属于 有 准备的 人。
Success belongs to those who are prepared.

词组：出于、限于、于是
Phrase: out of, limited to, so

92 回 huí Return

返回、循环、次数

Return, cycle, number of times

是 该 回家了。
It's time to go home.

回头 看 一眼。
Turning back for a glance.

回忆 往事，不甚 感慨。
Reflecting on the past, filled with deep emotions.

词组：回复、回响、回族
Phrase: reply, echo, Hui people

93 笑 xiào — Laugh

愉快的表情、欢喜的声音

A happy expression, a joyful voice

外面 传来 她的 欢笑声。
听到 笑话，他 忍不住 大笑。
笑的 是 她的 眼睛，口唇，和
唇边 浑圆的 漩涡。
词组：好笑、笑纳、嬉笑

Her laughter came from outside.
He couldn't help laughing at the joke.
Her laughter lies in her eyes, her lips, and
the rounded dimples beside her mouth.
Phrases: funny, accept with a smile,
playful laughter

94 所 suǒ — Place

具体场所、抽象归属

Specific place, abstract belonging

研究所 是 独立的。
博主 记录下了 旅程中 的 所见
所闻。
火警! 所有 人 必须 离开。
词组：所在、所谓、所以

The institute is independent.
The blogger recorded what he saw and
heard during the journey.
Fire! Everyone must leave.
Phrase: where, so called, so

95 但 dàn — But, only

连接前后语义对立、限定范围
或程度
他 虽 年轻，但 经验 丰富。
但凡 有 办法，我 必 尽力
但愿 人 长久。
词组：但是、不但、但且

Connect the semantic opposition before
and after, limit the scope or degree
He is young, but experienced.
I will try my best if there is a way.
Wishing for enduring togetherness.
Phrase: but, not only, if only

96 眼 yǎn — Eye

视觉器官、对事物的看法

Visual organs, views on things

眼睛 注视着 前方。
脚步 不能 达到 的 地方，眼光
可以 达到
活在 眼前。
词组：鹰眼、眼色、眼红

Eyes look ahead.
The vision can reach places that the feet
cannot reach.
Live in the present.
Phrase: eagle eyes, a meaningful glance,
jealous

97 成 chéng — Finish

完成、转换、成为的状态
Complete, transform, the state of becoming

他俩 成了 好朋友。
They became good friends.

这 学期 成绩 不好。
This semester, the grades were not good.

果园 里面 的 苹果 成熟 了 。
The apples in the orchard are ripe.

词组：成功、成就、成语
Phrases: success, achievement, idiom

98 方 fāng — Square

空间与几何、方法与规则
Space and geometry, methods and rules

正方形 有 四个 角。
A square has four corners.

太阳 从 东方 升起。
The sun rises in the east.

不同的 地方 有 不同的 方言。
Different places have different dialects.

词组：方向、方案、平方
Phrase: direction, plan, square

99 年 nián — Year

时间单位
Time unit

一年 有 365 天 。
There are 365 days in a year.

新年 快乐!
Happy New Year!

年青 就是 好。
Being young is good.

词组：年华、过年、年节
Phrases: time of youth, celebrate New Year, annual festivals

100 见 jiàn — See

看见、认知
See, cognition

视 而 不见。
To look but not see.

沙漠 治理 已经 见到 成效。
Desert control has yielded results.

初次 见面 就 看出 他 很 有 见解。
I saw he was very insightful when we first met.

词组：会见、见笑、见习
Phrases: meet, to cause amusement (in a humble way), apprentice

101 当 dāng

承担、表示时间和空间

儿子 长大 想 当 老师。
当 你 笑的 时候 全世界 都在笑。
小偷 被 当场 抓住。
词组：当家、当初、当地

Serve, at

To bear, to indicate time and space

My son wants to be a teacher when he grows up.
When you laugh, the whole world laughs.
The thief was caught on the spot.
Phrase: to be in charge, at the beginning, at the place

102 女 nǚ

女人、女性

女儿 生了 一个 女孩。
妇女 能 顶 半边天 。
女士 优先。
词组：女方、女婿、子女

Women

Woman, female

My daughter gave birth to a girl.
Women hold up half the sky.
Ladies first.
Phrase: female party, son-in-law, children

103 真 zhēn

真实、强调内在及感情

故事 是 真的 吗?
真相 只有 一个。
真情 值得 珍惜。
词组：真理、认真、真正

True

Real, emphasize inner and emotional

Is the story true?
There is only one truth.
True feelings are worth cherishing.
Phrase: truth, seriousness, real

104 两 liǎng

二、模糊数量、重量单位

两人 互不 相让。
过 两天 病 就好了。
1斤 等于 10两。
词组：两极、两难、两句

Two

Two，fuzzy quantity and weight units

The two people refused to give in to each other.
The illness will be cured in a few days.
1 jin is equal to 10 liang.
Phrases: two extremes, dilemma, a few words

105 力 lì　Force

肌肉的力、力量、效能　Muscle force, strength, efficiency

饿得 没 力气 了。
我 尽力 将 事情 做好。
牛顿 力学 第三 定律：作用力
与 反作用力 相等。
词组：体力、能力、视力

I am so hungry that I have no strength left.
I try my best to get things done.
Newton's third law of mechanics: action and reaction are equal.
Phrase: physical strength, ability, vision

106 气 qì　Gas

物质状态、流动的能量　State of matter, flowing energy

空气 是 一种 气体。
不要 气 我 了。
穿上 西装 好 气派。
词组：生气、气味、运气

Air is a gas.
Don't make me angry.
Putting on a suit gives such an air of authority.
Phrase: anger, smell, luck

107 从 cóng　From

跟随、顺服、起点和经由　Follow, obey, starting point and via

不管 什么 命令，你 都 服从?
从 杭州 到 南京 的 车票 还有 吗?
从 我 做起。
词组：从政、从何、从此

No matter what the order is, you obey it?
Are there any tickets from Hangzhou to Nanjing?
Start with me.
Phrases: enter politics, from where, from now on

108 用 yòng　Use

使用、工具或资源　Use, tools, or resources

用力 推。
费用 太 高 了。
有用 的 人 在 哪里 都 有用。
词组：用心、用品、用户

Push hard.
The cost is too high.
Useful people are useful everywhere.
Phrases: care, supplies, users

109 长 (1)zhǎng (2)cháng Grow, long

成长、延续　Growth, continuation

你 又 长¹ 高了。　You have grown taller.
做 什么 都 最好 有 长²远 规划。　It is best to have a long-term plan for everything you do.
你的 专长² 是 什么?　What is your specialty?
词组：增长¹、长²期、长²江　Phrase: growth, long-term, the Long River

110 动 dòng Move

用力使移动、变化　To move something with force, change

水面 出现 波动。　The water surface ripples.
他 很 容易 动怒。　He gets angry easily.
没电了，车 没了 动力。　Battery is dead, the car has no power.
词组：运动、动心、动作　Phrase: movement, to be tempted, action

111 间 jiān Between

空间间隔、时间区间、隔开　Spatial interval, time interval, separation

一个 房间 被 隔成 两个 小 房间。　A room is divided into two small rooms.
时间 过得 飞快。　Time flies.
辣椒 玉米 可以 间隔 套种。　Peppers and corn can be interplanted.
词组：间隙、田间、期间　Phrases: gap, field, period

112 国 guó Nation

政治实体、地域文化共同体　Political entity, regional cultural community

中国 的 全称 是 中华 人民 共和国。　The full name of China is the People's Republic of China.
联合国 维持 和平。　The United Nations maintains peace.
故国 不堪 回首 月明中 。　The homeland is unbearable to recall beneath the bright moon.
词组：国防、国籍、国际　Phrase: national defense, nationality, international

113 走 zǒu　Walk

步行、移动、趋向

Walk, move, trend

再 走 几步 就 到了。
钟 走 得 不准。
股市 走向 很难 预测。
词组：竞走、走漏、走红

Just a few more steps and we'll be there.
The clock is not running accurately.
The stock market trend is hard to predict.
Phrases: race walk, leak, become popular

114 让 ràng　Yield

礼让、允许

Courtesy, allow

各 让 一步，就 不 吵架 了。
谦让 是 美德。
让 我 试试。
词组：避让、忍让、转让

If both sides give in, there will be no quarrel.
Modesty and yielding are virtues.
Let me try.
Phrases: avoid, tolerate, transfer

115 被 bèi　Cover

覆盖身体、受动

Cover the body, passive

床上 有 一床 被子。
植被 被 破坏了。
他 被 老板 辞退 了。
词组：棉被、被动、被告

There is a quilt on the bed.
The vegetation was destroyed.
He was fired by his boss.
Phrase: quilt, passive, defendant

116 给 gěi　Give

提供、使对方得到、致使

To provide, to make the other party obtain, to cause

我 给你 一个 好评。
干嘛 给我 一顿 骂？
房子 给 火 烧掉了。
词组：送给、交给、供给(jǐ)

I give you a good review.
Why did you scold me?
The house was burned down by fire.
Phrase: give, hand over, supply

117 正 zhèng　Right

正确、纠正、正在　　Correct, to correct, in the process of

不是 正解。　　Not the correct answer.
正午 时分 天气 很热。　　It was very hot at noon.
领导 正在 开会。　　The leader is in a meeting.
词组：正义、正月、纯正　　Phrases: justice, first month, pure

118 问 wèn　Ask

询问、探求、问题本身　　Inquiry, explore, the question itself

我 帮 你 问过了。　　I asked for you.
警察 审问 了 罪犯。　　The police interrogated the criminal.
你 问 一句，他 答 一句。　　You ask a question, he answers a
词组：问题、问候、慰问　　question.
　　Phrases: question, greeting, condolence

119 打 dǎ　Hit

敲击、制作、从事活动　　To strike, to make, to engage in activities

谁 在 打铁?　　Who is forging iron?
给 爷爷 打个 电话。　　Give Grandpa a call.
大家 都是 打工人。　　We are all workers.
词组：打架、打印、打赌　　Phrases: to fight, to print, to bet

120 明 míng　Bright

光亮、清晰、照亮、理解　　Bright, clear, illuminate, understand

灯火 通明，照得 像 白昼 一样 明亮。　　The lights are bright, shining as bright as day.
我 明白了。　　I understand.
我 来 说明 一下。　　Let me explain.
词组：光明、明星、明说　　Phrases: bright, star, speak plainly

121 儿 ér

儿子、幼童、男子

儿子 已经 大学 毕业 了。
小孩儿 不懂事。
男儿 志 在 四方。
词组：儿女、女儿、儿媳

Son

Son, young child, man

Son has graduated from college.
Children are ignorant.
A man's ambition lies in the four corners
of the world.
Phrase: sons and daughters, daughter,
daughter-in-law

122 法 fǎ

刑律、规则、方法

违法 者 将 受到 法律 制裁。
一切 都 合法。
这个 算法 更好。
词组：法治、法庭、佛法

Law

Criminal law, rules, methods

Violators will be punished by law.
Everything is legal.
This algorithm is better.
Phrase: rule of law, court, Buddhism

123 才 cái

天赋与能力、具备能力的人、
仅仅
这人 很有 才干，是个 人才。
她 是 才貌 双全。
才 用了 三天 就 坏了。
词组：才能、口才、奴才

Ability

Talent and ability, capable person, only

This person is very capable, a talent.
She is both talented and beautiful.
It broke after only three days of use.
Phrases: talent, eloquence, slave

124 几 jǐ

小型、将近、不定的数目

茶几 古色 古香。
车 几乎 撞到 墙上。
来了 好 几百 人。
词组：几许、几率、几何

Almost, a few

Small, nearly, indefinite number

The tea table is quaint and classical
elegance.
The car almost hit the wall.
Hundreds of people came.
Phrase: how much, probability, geometry

125 行 (1)xíng (2)háng Go, line

(1) 移动、行为 (2) 道路、队列   (1) Move, act (2) Road, queue

邮轮 开始了 海上 航行[1]。   The cruise ship started its sea voyage.
行[1]动 才能 成功 。   Only action can lead to success.
IT 行[2]业仍需要人。   The IT industry still needs people.
词组：行[1]为、修行[1]、银行[2]   Phrase: action, spiritual practice, bank

126 三 sān Three

数字、次序、多次   Number, order, multiple times

一 加 二 等于 三。   One plus two equals three.
三人行，则 必有 我师。   When three people walk together, there must be one person who can teach me.
务必 三思 而行。   Think twice before you act.
词组：三角、三维、三国   Phrases: triangle, three-dimensional, Three Kingdoms

127 定 dìng Stable

安定、使稳定、稳固的   Stable, make stable, firm

确定了的事，就 不要 再变。   Once something is determined, don't change it.
机票 定 好了。   The plane ticket is booked.
不管 多危险，他 都 很 镇定。   No matter how dangerous it is, he is very calm.
词组：定律、定论、坚定   Phrase: natural law, conclusion, firmness

128 此 cǐ This

指代近处或当前、强调当下   Refers to the near or present, emphasizes the present

此路 不 通。   This road is blocked.
就 到此 为止 吧。   Let's stop here.
此生 无 憾。   No regrets in this life.
词组：彼此、此刻、此地   Phrase: each other, now, here

129 进 jìn

移动、提升

前面 是 商城，进去 看看。
今年 她的 成绩 有 进步。
明天 需要 进货。
词组：进退、进行、进程

Advance

Move, improve

There is a mall in front, go in and have a look.
Her grades have improved this year.
We need to restock tomorrow.
Phrase: advance and retreat, proceed, process

130 再 zài

重复、延续、进一步

再见。
再 打 一局。
再 不 走 就要 迟到 了。
词组：再次、再说、再三

Again

Repeat, continue, further

See you later.
Play one more round.
If you don't leave now, you'll be late.
Phrases: once again, talk about it later, again and again

131 种 (1)zhǒng(2)zhòng

(1) 种子、种类 (2) 种植

每种¹ 植物 都 留点 种¹子。
他 各种¹各样 的 角色 都 演过。
花园 里 也 可以 种²点 菜。
词组：种¹族、物种¹、种²地

Seed, to plant

(1) Seeds, species (2) Planting

Leave some seeds for each plant.
He has played a variety of roles.
You can also plant some vegetables in the garden.
Phrases: race, species, planting

132 将 (1)jiàng (2)jiāng

(1) 军事统领 (2) 时间指向、行为引导

他的 军衔 是 中将¹。
将²来 会 更 美好。
将² 门 关好。
词组：将¹领、将²要、将²就

General, will

(1) Military command (2) Time direction, behavior guidance

His military rank is Lieutenant General.
Things will be better in the future.
Close the door.
Phrases: commander, will, make do

133 实 shí　True
充满、真实

Full, real

粮仓 充实 了，人们 才 能 懂得 礼节 。
这个人 很 实在。
UFO 是 不 真实的。
词组：果实、实验、事实

People will learn etiquette only when the granary is full.
This person is very sincere.
UFOs are not real.
Phrase: fruit, experiment, fact

134 同 tóng　Same
表示重复和一致

Indicates repetition and agreement

我 同意 你的 想法。
我们 一同 生活，一同 成长。
我们 几个 同学 同岁。
词组：相同、同样、共同

I agree with your idea.
We live together and grow up together.
Several of us classmates are the same age.
Phrase: same, same kind, shared

135 最 zuì　Most
首要的、顶点

First, apex

最好 还是 坐 高铁。
最后 还是 坐了 高铁。
这个 函数 有 最大值。
词组：最初、最佳、之最

It is better to take the high-speed rail.
In the end, I took the high-speed rail.
This function has a maximum value.
Phrase: first, best, the best of

136 本 běn　Root
草木的根、根基、主体

The root of plants, foundation, and main part

我们 应从 根本 上 去 解决 这个 问题。
本钱 都 亏掉 了。
人的 本性 是 自私的。
词组：书本、本校、本质

We should solve this problem from the root.
All the capital has been lost.
Human nature is selfish.
Phrase: book, my school, essence

137 向 xiàng — Toward

朝向、目标、趋近

Towards, goal, approach

海景房 面向 大海。
他 向 我们 走来 。
人们 向往 自由 。
词组：方向、向导、倾向

The sea view room faces the sea.
He is walking towards us.
People yearn for freedom.
Phrase: direction, guide, tendency

138 分 fēn — Divide

分割、部分和界限、时间单位

Division, part and boundary, time unit

分数 是 把 一个 单位 平均 分成 几份 。
失败 后 要 分析 原因。
还有 五 分钟 就 十点。
词组：分界、区分、分手

Fractions are to divide a unit into several equal parts.
After failure, we need to analyze the reasons.
There are five minutes to ten o'clock.
Phrase: divide, distinguish, break up

139 十 shí — Ten

数字、表示齐全

Number, indicating completeness

一个 月 大约 三十 天。
没有 人 十全十美，除了 你。
十分 之一 等于 百分 之十。
词组：十指、十字架、十分

A month is about thirty days.
No one is perfect, except you.
One tenth is equal to ten percent.
Phrases: ten fingers, cross, very

140 学 xué — Learn

知识获取、教育、模仿

Knowledge acquisition, education, imitation

他 在 大学 学 数学。
孩子 学 狗 叫。
他的学位 是 化学 学士。
词组：学习、学生、学术

He is studying mathematics at university.
The child learned to bark like a dog.
His degree is a bachelor's degree in chemistry.
Phrase: study, student, academic

141 高 gāo — High

垂直距离大 、地位或境界

Large vertical distance, status or realm

高原 气压 低。
高! 就是高!
一高兴 忘了 自己 有 高血压
。
词组：高楼、高级、高度

The air pressure on the plateau is low.
Smart! Really smart!
When I was happy, I forgot that I had high blood pressure.
Phrases: high-rise, high-level, height

142 第 dì — No.

表示次序、等级或特定身份

Indicates order, rank or specific status

第一名 又叫 冠军。
在 山上 第三天 他 生病了。
第二次 世界 大战 中国 也是
战场。
词组：第一手 、门第、第几

The first place is also called the champion.
On the third day in the mountain, he fell ill.
China was also a battlefield during World War II.
Phrases: first-hand, family background, which number

143 感 gǎn — Feel

感知外界、情感共鸣、互动

Perceiving the outside world, emotional resonance, interaction

感觉 有点 冷 。
感恩 是 基督徒的 一种 生活
态度。
也许 是 传感器 的 问题。
词组：感谢、感动、痛感

Feeling a little cold.
Gratitude is a way of life for Christians.
Maybe it's a sensor problem.
Phrases: gratitude, moving, feeling pain

144 怎 zěn — How

询问方式、原因或状况

Inquiry method, reason or situation

这个 问题 怎么 解决?
怎么 就 忘记了?
不管 怎样，我们 不能 退缩。
词组：怎能、怎么办、怎不

How to solve this problem?
How did you forget it?
No matter what, we can't back down.
Phrase: how can, how to, why not

145 神 shén — Spirit

超自然的存在、灵性及非凡

Supernatural existence, spirituality and extraordinary

世人 都说 神仙 好。
幸福 是 风中 期待的 眼神。
神经 系统 非常 复杂。
词组：财神、神秘、心神

People of the world all say immortals are good.
Happiness is the gaze of anticipation in the wind.
The nervous system is very complex.
Phrase: God of wealth, mysterious, mind

146 听 tīng — Hear

声音和信息的接收

Reception of sounds and information

中文 听力 有 进步。
她 在 听 音乐，没 听见 你 喊 她。
她 听从 了 医生 的 建议。
词组：听觉、听众、倾听

Chinese listening skills have improved.
She was listening to music and didn't hear you calling her.
She followed the doctor's advice.
Phrases: hearing, audience, listening

147 边 biān — Edge

空间与抽象界限

Space and abstract boundaries

多边形 有 多条 边 。
很多 城市 都 建在 河边 。
他 身边的 人 都是 好 朋友。
词组：边界、边上、边缘

A polygon has many sides.
Many cities are built along rivers.
The people around him are all good friends.
Phrases: boundary, edge, margin

148 作 zuò — Make

制造、从事、身份和成果

Make, engage in, identity and results

他的 工作 就是 作画。
作家 的 作品 很 受 欢迎。
不 作死 就 不会 死 。
词组：作业、作用、作证

His job is to paint.
The writer's work is very popular.
If you don't court death, you won't die.
Phrase: homework, role, testify

149 其 qí

That

指代第三人称、事物、范围

Refers to the third person, thing, scope

其他人都走了？
每个人都有其独特的才能。
这座城市以其美丽的风景闻名。
词组：其实、其余、其中

Have all the others left?
Everyone has his or her own unique talent.
This city is famous for its beautiful scenery.
Phrases: in fact, the rest, among them

150 吧 ba

语气助词、缓和语气

Tone particle, softening tone

他应该到家了吧？
别生气了吧，这样总行了吧？
算了吧，就这样吧。
词组：行吧、是吧、对吧

He should be home, right?
Don't be angry, is this good enough now?
Forget it, let's just leave it like this.
Phrase: OK, yeah, right

151 却 què

Retreat, but

退避、语义转折

Retreat, semantic transition

面对那么多的困难，他却步不前。
我来了，他却走了。
看似简单，却不简单。
词组：退却、忘却、却是

Faced with so many difficulties, he hesitated to move forward.
I came, but he left.
It seems simple, but it is not.
Phrase: retreat, forget, but it is

152 口 kǒu

Mouth

嘴巴、开口、用口表达

Mouth, opening, expressing with mouth

口渴需要喝水？
伤口好了吗？
他口头同意了。
词组：瓶口、港口、口袋

Are you thirsty and need to drink water?
Is the wound healed?
He verbally agreed.
Phrase: bottle mouth, port, pocket

153 觉 (1)jiào (2)jué   Sleep, feel

(1) 睡眠状态 (2) 认知的觉醒

(1) Sleeping state (2) Cognitive awakening

我 睡了 一 觉[1]。
觉[2]得 头 有点 晕。
我 喜欢 舒服 的 感觉[2]。
词组：听觉[2]、觉[2]察、睡觉[1]

I took a nap.
I felt a little dizzy.
I like the feeling of comfort.
Phrases: hearing, awareness, sleep

154 啊 ā

语气、不同声调表达不同情感

Different tones and intonations express different emotions

啊 (ā)，真美!
啊 (á)? 你说什么?
啊 (ǎ)? 这是真的吗?
啊 (à)! 原来是这样!
你说的是他啊 (a)。

Ah, so beautiful!
Ah? What did you say?
Ah? Is this true?
Ah! So that's it!
You're talking about him.

155 因 yīn   Cause

事物的根源与条件

The root and condition of things

霜冻 是 小麦 减产 的 原因。
演出 因雨 延期 。
因为 有你，阳光 灿烂。
词组：因而、病因、因果

Frost is the reason for the reduction in wheat production.
The performance was postponed due to rain.
Because of you, the sun is shining.
Phrase: therefore, cause of illness, cause and effect

156 白 bái   White

颜色、清楚、说清楚

Color, clear, make it clear

我 还是 喜欢 吃 白 米饭。
相信 你 是 清白的。
自白 是 自我 表白 的 意思。
词组：白纸、白雪、蛋白

I still like to eat white rice.
I believe you are innocent.
Confession means self-declaration.
Phrase: white paper, white snow, egg white (protein)

157 次 cì — Order

排列的位序、质量差

Ranking order, poor quality

一次是偶然，两次是或然，三次是必然。
次品 减价 百分之五十。
名次 决 出来了 吗?
词组: 层次、首次、次日

Once is accidental, twice is possible, three times is inevitable.
Defective products are discounted by 50%.
Has the ranking been decided?
Phrases: level, first time, next day

158 军 jūn — Military

武装力量及相关

Armed Forces and Related

军队 对 军人 要求 很 严。
今年 新 产品 发布，全军 覆没。
盟军 在 诺曼底 登陆。
词组: 军长、军训、从军

The army has very strict requirements for soldiers.
This year's new product launch resulted in total failure.
The Allied forces landed in Normandy.
Phrase: army commander, military training, join military

159 做 zuò — Make

制造、从事、装扮

Make, engage in, act as

我 来 做饭。
别人 不能 替你 做 决定。
她 做了 一个 鬼脸。
词组: 做人、做伴、做客

I'll cook.
Others can't make decisions for you.
She made a face.
Phrases: be a person, be a companion, be a guest

160 外 wài — Out

空间的表层或外围、界限

The surface or periphery of a space, boundaries

穿 件 外套，门外 很冷。
送 外卖 的 在 外面 等你。
外交 是 内政 的 延续。
词组: 外企、外语、见外

Put on a coat, it's cold outside.
The delivery is waiting for you outside.
Diplomacy is a continuation of domestic affairs.
Phrase: foreign companies, foreign language, don't be so formal

161 门 mén

Gate

建筑出入口、途径、派别

Building entrances, paths, factions

城门 敞开着。
问 问题 是 一门 学问 。
当 上帝 关了 这 扇门，一定
会 为你 打开 另 一扇门 。
词组：门卫、门路、门生

The city gate is wide open.
Asking questions is an art.
When God closes this door, he will
definitely open another one for you.
Phrases: gatekeeper, way, disciple

162 光 guāng

Light

可见辐射、明亮、增辉

Visible radiation, bright, radiant

窗前 明 月光，疑是 地上 霜。
最好的 时光，总是 特别 短 。
结了 冰 的 马路 很 光滑 。
词组：光荣、火光、光泽

Before my bed, the bright moonlight, I
suspect it is frost on the ground.
The best time is always very short.
The icy road is very smooth.
Phrase: glory, fire, luster

163 风 fēng

Wind

空气流动、潮流、景象

Air flow, trend, scene

送 你 三月的 风、六月的
雨、九月的 风景。
近来 流行 复古 风潮。
听到 什么 风声?
词组：风暴、风气、台风

Give you the wind of March, the rain of
June, and the scenery of September.
Recently, retro style is popular.
What rumor do you hear?
Phrase: storm, culture, typhoon

164 主 zhǔ

Master

所有者、掌控、核心

Owner, control, core

谁 是 一家 之主?
你 能 作主? 别 自作 主张。
她 是 整场 戏 的 主角。
词组：主要、主义、主持

Who is the head of the family?
Can you make the decision? Don't take it
upon yourself.
She is the leading role of the entire play.
Phrase: main, doctrine, preside over

165 住 zhù

居留、停止

伟杰 住校，浩宇 住在 家里。
我 忍不住 笑了 。
记住，遵守 交通 规则 。
词组：住处、住户、住手

Reside, stop

Residence, stop

Weijie lives in school, Haoyu lives at home.
I couldn't help laughing.
Remember to obey traffic rules.
Phrases: residence, resident, stop

166 果 guǒ

果实 、结果、决断

苹果、奇异果、火龙果、百香果 都是 水果。
实验 结果 是 可信的。
广告 的 效果 超出 预期 。
词组：果汁、因果、恶果

Fruit

Fruit, result, decision

Apple, kiwi, dragon fruit, passion fruit are all fruits.
The experimental results are credible.
The effect of the advertisement exceeded expectations.
Phrases: juice, cause and effect, bad result

167 与 yǔ

表示并列或共同关系、给予、参与

我 与 他 是 朋友。
我 必 与 你 同在 。
与人 方便 与己 方便。
词组：赠与、与其

And

Indicates parallel or common relationship, giving, participation

I am friends with him.
I will be surely with you.
Help others, and you help yourself.
Phrase: give, rather than

168 全 quán

完整、周全

全 世界 都 为之 震惊。
所有 的 人 全 来了。
我们 一定 全力 以赴。
词组：全体、完全、保全

Whole

Complete, comprehensive

The whole world was shocked.
Everyone came.
We must do our best.
Phrase: whole, complete, preservation

169 二 èr — Two

数字、次序

Number, order

第二名 叫 亚军。
老王 说一 不二 。
祖孙 二人 走在 沙滩上。
词组：二手、二意、二房

The second place is called runner-up.
Lao Wang is a man of his word.
The grandfather and grandson walked on the beach.
Phrases: second-hand, two minds, second wife

170 侯 hòu — Wait

等待、看望、时节

Waiting, visiting, season

候车室 非常 拥挤。
代我 问候 你 爸爸。
气候 变暖。
词组：等候、时候、候鸟

The waiting room is very crowded.
Give your father my regards.
The climate is getting warmer.
Phrase: waiting, time, migratory birds

171 公 gōng — Fair

平分、公平、公正

Equal distribution, fairness, justice

法律 是 公正的。
公民 有 受 教育的 权利。
数学 公式 常 简称为 公式。
词组：公开、公安、公子

The law is fair.
Citizens have the right to education.
Mathematical formulas are often referred to as formulas.
Phrase: public, public security, son

172 相 (1)xiàng (2)xiāng — Photo，mutual

(1) 审视、容貌 (2) 交互

(1) to examine, appearance (2) to interact

大家 一起 照张相[1]。
小女孩 相[1]貌 清秀。
我们 相[2]识 十多年。
词组：相[1]片、首相[1]、相[2]爱

Let's take a photo together.
The little girl has a pretty face.
We have known each other for more than ten years.
Phrase: photo, prime minister, love each other

173 吗 ma

疑问助词

这是 你的 房子吗?
真的吗? 不 可能吧!
难道 你 不 明白吗?

Interrogative particle

Is this your house?
Really? Impossible!
Don't you understand?

174 等 děng

量相同、级别、等候

人人 生 而 平等。
1 加 1 等于 2.
值得 拥有的 都 值得 等待。
词组: 等级、等价、头等

Equal

Equal quantity, level, waiting

All men are born equal.
1 plus 1 equals 2.
What is worth having is worth waiting for.
Phrases: level, equal value, first class

175 别 bié

分离、区分、禁止

分别 十年的 好友 又 相见。
我 看不出 两者 的 区别。
别 这样, 这样 不好。
词组: 离别、辨别、类别

Separate

Separate, distinguish, prohibit

Good friends who have been separated for ten years meet again.
I can't see the difference between the two.
Don't do this, it's not good.
Phrases: separation, distinguish, category

176 色 sè

性欲、颜色、表情

老板 好色, 经常 性骚扰 女 员工。
印象派的 画 色彩 丰富。
李强 面露 喜色, 一定 有 好 消息。
词组: 彩色、气色、景色

Color

Sexual desire, color, expression

The boss is lustful and often sexually harasses female employees.
Impressionist paintings are rich in color.
Li Qiang looks happy, so there must be good news.
Phrase: color, complexion, scenery

177 死 sǐ

Die

生命终止、丧失功能、固执

End of life, loss of function, stubbornness

人死了，不能 复生。
计算机 死机 了。
他 很 死板，进了 死 胡同，也 不 回头。
词组：死人、死火山、死战

Once a person dies, he cannot be resurrected.
The computer crashed.
He is very rigid, even if he has reached a dead end, he will not turn back.
Phrase: dead person, dead volcano, fight until death

178 张 zhāng

Expand

扩大、布置、姓

Expand, arrange, surname

这家 店 新 开张。
张 先生 说的 有点 夸张。
中美 关系 比较 紧张。
词组：扩张、张罗、张望

This store is newly opened.
What Mr. Zhang said is a bit exaggerated.
Sino-US relations are quite tense.
Phrases: expand, arrange, look around

179 部 bù

Division

单位、安排

Unit, Arrangement

人事部 是 负责 招聘、培训、和 管理的 部门。
部队 到达了 指点 地点。
部署 没有 问题。
词组：外部、部下、部分

The HR department is responsible for recruitment, training, and management.
The troops arrived at the designated location.
The deployment has no issues.
Phrase: external, subordinates, part

180 太 tài

Very

极大、极端

Great, extreme

中国 古代 崇拜 太阳 神。
太空 旅行 已是 现实。
电视剧 太长了，谁看得完？
词组：太平、太多、太太

Ancient China worshipped the sun god.
Space travel is a reality.
The TV series is too long, who can finish it?
Phrase: peaceful, too much, wife

181 日 rì — Sun

太阳、白天、一天

Sun, daytime, day

日月星辰，有你 日日 与我 相伴。
明日 复 明日，明日 何其 多?
日本 的 国旗 是 太阳 旗。
词组：红日、日程、日出

Sun, moon, stars, you accompany me every day.
Tomorrow after tomorrow, how many tomorrows are there?
Japanese national flag is the sun flag.
Phrase: red sun, schedule, sunrise

182 少 (1)shǎo (2)shào — Less，young

(1) 数量微小、短缺 (2) 年龄小

(1) Small quantity or shortage (2) Young age

各家的 烦恼 都 不少[1]。
公司 缺少[1] 客户，要 倒闭 了。
少[2]年时 爱好 学习。
词组：少[1]数、少[2]女

Every family has its own troubles.
The company lacks customers and is going to close down.
When I was young, I loved studying.
Phrases: a few, girl

183 站 zhàn — War

武力冲突、激烈竞争、直立

Armed conflict, fierce competition, upright

战争 是 要 死人的。
商场 如 战场。
卫兵 站立 在门前 一动不动。
词组：战术、车站、挑战

War inevitably causes deaths.
The business world is like a battlefield.
The guard stood in front of the door motionless.
Phrase: tactics, station, challenge

184 理 lǐ — Logic

玉石纹理、整理、规律

Jade texture, organize, rules

她 的 建议 很有 道理。
工商 管理 是 一门 综合性 学科。
他 做事 有条有理。
词组：物理、理论、理想

Her suggestion makes a lot of sense.
Business administration is a multidisciplinary field.
He does things in an orderly and methodical manner.
Phrase: physics, theory, ideal

185 直 zhí — Straight

不弯曲、伸开、正直

Unbend, stretch, integrity

可以 用 直尺 画 一条 直线。
这条 路 一直 通向 市 中心。
我 直接 告诉 他 不行。
词组：直言、直径 、 耿直

Can draw a straight line with a ruler.
This road leads straight to the city center.
I directly told him no.
Phrase: straight talk, diameter, honest

186 重 (1)zhòng(2)chóng — Heavy，again

(1) 分量大、重要 (2) 重复

(1) heavy, important (2) repetitive

太 重[1] 了，我 拿 不动。
重[1]要 的 事情 要 重[2]复 三 遍。
能力 越大，责任 越重[1]。
词组：重[1]伤、重[1]视、重[2]庆

It's too heavy, I can't lift it.
Important things should be repeated three times.
With great power, comes great responsibility.
Phrases: seriously injured, attach importance, Chongqing

187 王 wáng — King

最高统治者、最强者、姓氏

Supreme ruler, strongest, surname

王侯将 相 今 何 在？
竞争 中，胜者 为王。
蜂王 是 一个 蜂群 的 首领，永远 是 雌蜂 。
词组：国王、王后、称王

Where are the kings and generals now?
In competition, the winner is the king.
The queen bee is the leader of a bee colony and is always a female bee.
Phrases: king, queen, become king

188 像 xiàng — Figure

人类形象、图像、比方

Human image, image, such as

画像 画得 很 像。
镜子 里 看到 的 是 镜像。
像 我 这样 优秀 的 人 一定 会 成功。
词组：肖像、雕像、好像

The portrait is very lifelike.
What you see in the mirror is the mirror image.
A person as good as me will definitely succeed.
Phrase: portrait, statue, like

189 脸 liǎn

面部、尊严、表面

Face

Face, dignity, surface

孩子 发烧，脸色 通红。
丢脸的 事 我 不做。
太阳 刚 露脸的 时候，我 也
起床了。
词组：红过脸、笑脸

The child has a fever and his face is red.
I don't do shameful things.
When the sun just came out, I got up.
Phrases: had a quarrel, smiling face

190 比 bǐ

并列、比较

Compare

Juxtapose, comparison

足球 比赛 结果：四 比 二。
经过 反复 比较，还是 决定 用
红色。
他 比 我 胖 六 公斤。
词组：比例、对比、比喻

Football match result: 4 to 2.
After repeated comparisons, we decided
to use red.
He is six kilograms fatter than me.
Phrases: proportion, contrast, metaphor

191 快 kuài

畅快、利落、速度高

Quick

Joyful, neat, fast

祝 生日 快乐!
他 快人 快语，同事 都 喜欢
他。
这么 快? 上午 的 快寄，下午
就 到了。
词组：赶快、痛快、快事

Happy birthday!
He is a straightforward person and his
colleagues like him.
So fast? The express mail in the morning
arrived in the afternoon.
Phrases: hurry, joyful, pleasant events

192 何 hé

疑问代词

What

Interrogative pronouns

赵本山 是 何人?
春花 秋月 何时 了?
都是 邻居，何必 如此 争吵?
词组：何不、何如、何苦

Who is Zhao Benshan?
When will the spring blossoms and
autumn moon come to an end?
We are all neighbors, why do we have to
quarrel like this?
Phrase: why not, how about, why bother

193 水 shuǐ — Water

水、水体、液体和流动状态

Water, water bodies, liquids and flow states

水杯 里 没有 水 了。
海水 不是 淡水，是 咸水。
水银 是 一种 金属。
词组：水库、流水、洪水

There is no water in the cup.
Seawater is not fresh water, it is salt water.
Mercury is a metal.
Phrases: reservoir, flowing water, flood

194 名 míng — Name

称谓、声誉

Title, reputation

除了 正式 姓名 外，父母 常常 给 孩子 起 一个 小名。
名人 一般 很 注重 他们 的 名声。
你的 名字 不在 名单 中。
词组：名称、名次、名利

In addition to their formal names, parents often give their children nicknames.
Celebrities are usually very concerned about their reputation.
Your name is not on the list.
Phrases: name, rank, fame and fortune

195 体 tǐ — Body

身体、事物、状态、风格

Body, thing, state, style

身体 是 革命 的 本钱。
水 可以 是 固体、液体 和 气体。
售后 服务 体系 需要 改进。
词组：体格、群体、体积

The body is the capital of revolution.
Water can be solid, liquid and gas.
The after-sales service system needs to be improved.
Phrases: physique, group, volume

196 呢 ne

语气助词，表示疑问、肯定、进行

A particle of mood, expressing doubt, affirmation, and progress.

你 干 什么 呢？我 正 吃饭 呢。
他 还 没来 呢。
今年 呢，比 去年 销量 好。

What are you doing? I'm eating.
He hasn't come yet.
This year, sales are better than last year.

197 东 dōng East

日出方向、主人

Sunrise direction, owner

大江 东 去。
东北人 豪爽。
你 把 钥匙 还给 房东 了吗?
词组: 东西、广东、东海

The great river flows eastward.
Northeastern people are bold and forthright.
Have you returned the key to the landlord?
Phrases: thing, Guangdong, East China Sea

198 叫 jiào Call

呼喊、命名、召唤

Shout, to name, summon

叫喊声 在 山间 回响。
你 叫 什么 名字?
叫 他 和 我们 一起 去。
词组: 叫好、吼叫、叫卖

The shouts echoed through the mountains.
What is your name?
Tell him to go with us.
Phrase: cheer, roar, hawking

199 西 xī West

太阳落下的一边

The side where the sun sets

西边的 太阳 就要 落山了。
山东省 和 山西省 不 相邻。
西方 文明 给 中国 带来了 西医、西装、西餐。
词组: 西藏、西红柿、西天

The sun is about to set in the west.
Shandong Province and Shanxi Province are not adjacent.
Western civilization brought Western medicine, Western suits, and Western food to China.
Phrases: Tibet, tomatoes, Western Paradise

200 应 (1)yìng (2)yīng Answer, should

(1) 回答 (2) 理该

(1) answer (2) should

你 答应了? 那 你 应该 去。
外国 客人 是 应邀 而来的。
他俩 之间 没有 化学 反应。
词组: 应对、呼应、应该

You agreed? Then you should go.
The foreign guests came on invitation.
There is no chemistry between them.
Phrase: respond, echo, should

201 便 biàn — Ease

安适、顺利、屎尿

Comfortable, smooth, shit and urine

那个 穿 便服的 是个 便衣 警察。
回来的 路上 顺便 去了 便利店。
随便 你，我 都行。
词组：便条、便于、便秘

The man in plain clothes is a plainclothes policeman.
On the way back, we stopped by a convenience store.
It's up to you, I'm fine with it.
Phrases: note, convenient for, constipation

202 放 fàng — Release

驱逐到远方、解脱约束

Drive away to a distant place, free from restraint

牧民们 哪里 有 水 和 草 就到 哪里 去 放牧。
放学了，我 去 玩 游戏。
人 要 拿得起，更要 放得下。
词组：放任、释放、放光

The herders go to graze wherever there is water and grass.
After school, I go to play games.
One must be able to pick things up, but even more importantly, let them go.
Phrases: let go, release, shine

203 马 mǎ — Horse

马匹、姓

Horse, surname

已经 在 马路上，马上 到。
祝你 马到 成功!
回族 人 很多 姓 马。
词组：马力、马戏、马来西亚

Already on the road, will arrive soon.
May you achieve instant success!
Many Hui people have the surname Ma.
Phrase: horsepower, circus, Malaysia

204 难 (1)nán (2)nàn — Difficult

(1) 不容易 (2) 灾祸、质问

(1) Not easy (2) Disaster, questioning

这个 问题 有点 难¹度。
人人 都有 困难¹的 时候。
难²民 需要 面对的 不仅仅 是 自然 灾难²。
词组：难¹处、难¹看、遭难²

This question is a bit difficult.
Everyone has difficult times.
Refugees have to face more than just natural disasters.
Phrase: difficulty, ugly, suffering

205 轻 qīng

Ease

轻便、分量小、不重要

Light, small, unimportant

我 轻轻 的 打开 房门。
年轻 时，不 懂事。
祖父 轻度 中风。
词组：轻便、轻松、轻声

I opened the door gently.
When I was young, I didn't know much.
My grandfather had a mild stroke.
Phrase: light, easy, soft voice

206 更 gèng

Alter, more

改变、程度递进

Change, progressive degree

年历 每年 需要 更新。
国家 足球队 又 更换 了 主教练。
明天 会 更 好。
词组：更改、更加、变更

The calendar needs to be updated every year.
The national football team has changed its head coach again.
Tomorrow will be better.
Phrases: change, more, alter

207 美 měi

Good

好吃、好看、高兴、称赞

Delicious, beautiful, happy, praise

她 很 爱美。
马先生 和 马太太 的 婚姻 很 美满。
请 帮忙 美言 几句。
词组：美术、美丽、美州

She loves beauty.
Mr. Ma and Mrs. Ma have a happy marriage.
Please help say a few kind words.
Phrase: art, beauty, America

208 位 wèi

Position

所在地方、等级、坐标

Location, level, coordinates

你 在 哪里? 告诉 我 你 的 位置。
座位 号 在 椅子 上方。
贡献 大 的 人 并 不一定 职位 高。
词组：位于、上位、单位

Where are you? Tell me your location.
The seat number is above the chair.
People who contribute a lot are not necessarily in high positions.
Phrases: located, rise in rank, unit

209 关 guān — Close

门闩、关卡、重要节点、牵挂
Latch, checkpoint, important node, worry

快 关上 窗子。
Close the window quickly.

要 上 大学 必须 过 高考 这 一关。
To go to college, you must pass the college entrance examination.

谢谢 你的 关心，我 已经 过了 鬼门关。
Thank you for your concern, I have already passed through the gate of hell.

词组：关押、海关、关节
Phrase: Detention, customs, joints

210 机 jī — Machine

枢要、机械、关键
Pivotal, machinery, key

客机 在 机场 安全 降落。
The plane landed safely at the airport.

危机 也是 机遇。
Crisis is also an opportunity.

你在 政府 机关 工作?
Do you work in the government?

词组：机密、机智、机器
Phrases: confidential, wit, machine

211 接 jiē — Receive

收取、连接、延续
Receive, connect, continue

地球 接受 到了 外星人 的 信号。
The earth received the alien signal.

4x100 米 接力 我们 赢了。
We won the 4x100m relay.

中国 与 俄国 接壤。
China borders Russia.

词组：接班、接待、接吻
Phrase: take over, reception, kiss

212 先 xiān — Prior

位置或时间在前
Position or time comes first

你 先 走吧，我 等 一会儿。
You go first, I'll wait for a while.

先 谢谢 您了!
Thank you in advance!

莫奈 是 现代 印象派 的 先驱 之一。
Monet is one of the pioneers of modern impressionism.

词组：先生、先前、先知
Phrases: Mr., predecessor, prophet

213 文 wén — Word

文身、文字及相关

Tattoos, writing and related

中文 最初 只是 象形文字。
你的 文章 很 严谨。
文史馆 的 文物 非常 珍贵。
词组：文化、文凭、天文

Chinese was initially just pictographic characters.
Your article is very rigorous.
The cultural relics in the Museum of Literature and History are precious.
Phrase: culture, diploma, astronomy

214 处 (1)chù (2)chǔ — Place

(1) 地方 (2) 安排、交往、惩罚

(1) Place (2) Arrangement, interact, punishment

住处¹离 办事处¹不远。
违反 规定 必须 严肃 处¹理。
与 人 相处²首先 要 尊重 人。
词组：好处¹、处¹事、处²决

Residence is not far from the office.
Violations of regulations must be dealt with seriously.
When dealing with people, you must first respect them.
Phrases: benefit, handling, execution

215 并 bìng — Merge, and

合为、递进或并列、加强否定语气

Merge, progression or parallelism, strengthen the negative tone

他两 并排 走来。
他工作努力，并取得了好成绩。
实际 并 不像 说的 那么好。
词组：合并、并存、并且

They walked side by side to us.
He worked hard and achieved good results.
The reality is not as good as it sounds.
Phrase: merge, coexist, furthermore

216 望 wàng — Look

看远处、观察、期盼

Look far, observe, look forward to

举头 望 明月。
一眼 望去 看不见 公司 的 未来。
我 希望 我们 可以 像 年轻时 那样 。
词组：张望、渴望、看望

Raising my head, I gaze at the bright moon.
Looking ahead, I can't see the company's future.
I hope we can be like we were when we were young.
Phrase: look around, desire, visit

217 常 cháng — Constant, often

规律、不变的、经常、普通

Regular pattern, unchanging, frequent, common

点石 成金，不合 常理。
历史 经常 重演。
常人 输了 会 生气，也是 人之 常情。
词组：常数、时常、反常

Turning stone into gold is unreasonable.
History often repeats itself.
It is normal for ordinary people to get angry when they lose.
Phrase: constant, often, abnormal

218 完 wán — Complete

完整、结束

Complete, finished

完了，完了!
任务 完成了吗?
他 做什么 都 追求 完美。
词组：完全、完人、完毕

It's over, it's over!
Is the mission completed?
He pursues perfection in everything he does.
Phrase: complete, perfect person, finished

219 四 sì — Four

数词

Numerals

春 夏 秋 冬 一年 四季。
四面、四处、四方 都表示 各 个 方向。
五环 你 比 四环 多 一环 。
词组：四门、四壁

Spring, summer, autumn and winter are the four seasons of the year.
Four sides, everywhere and four directions all refer to all directions.
Five rings, you have one more ring than four rings.
Phrases: four doors, four walls

220 飞 fēi — Fly

鸟在空中、飞行、快速

Birds in the air, flying, fast

雪花 飘飞。
飞流 直下 三千 尺。
不要 相信 流言 飞语。
词组：飞行、飞奔、双飞

Snowflakes flying.
The waterfall falls three thousand feet straight down.
Don't believe rumors.
Phrase: flying, running, flying in pairs

221 师 shī — Teacher

军队、传授知识的人、专业人士

Army, person who imparts knowledge, professional

军队 出师 不利。
The army started off badly.

师傅 是 一对一 传授 技能 的 老师。
A master is a teacher who imparts skills one-on-one.

工程师 按时 完成 了 设计。
The engineer completed the design on time.

词组：师长、师父、药剂师
Phrases: division commander, master, pharmacist

222 者 zhě — -er

助词，构成名词性短语
Particles, forming nominal phrases

作者 写得 不 清楚，读者 看 不懂。
The author did not write clearly, and the readers could not understand.

行者 匆匆。
The traveler hurries on.

智者 自知，仁者 自爱。
The wise know themselves, and the benevolent love themselves.

词组：学者、老者、记者
Phrase: scholar, old man, reporter

223 安 ān — Peaceful

平静、稳定、使安定
Calm, stable, make stable

祝 好人 一生 平安。
Wish good people a peaceful life.

也到 安家 立业 的 时候了。
It's also time to settle down and establish a career.

保安 保护 小区 的 安全。
Security guards protect the safety of the community.

词组：安排、安详、安装
Phrases: arrange, peaceful, install

224 清 qīng — Clear

洁净、明晰、廉洁
Clean, clear, integrity

清泉 石上 流。
A clear spring flows over rocks.

街上 没人，冷冷 清清。
The street is deserted, cold and quiet.

最近 忙于 清理 账目。
Recently busy with clearing accounts.

词组：清算、清香、清秀
Phrase: resolve, delicate fragrance, delicate and pretty

225 刚 gāng — Strong, just

坚硬、坚强、时间上紧接

Hard, strong, close in time

他 性格 刚直。
钻石 是 由 金刚石 加工 而成。
你 到的 刚刚 好。
词组：刚强、阳刚、刚才

He has an upright and forthright character.
Gem diamonds are made from diamonds.
You arrived just in time.
Phrase: strong, masculine, just now

226 跟 gēn — Heel, follow

脚后跟、随在后面、表示共同

Heel, following behind, indicating common

她 穿着 一双 高跟鞋。
干嘛 老 跟着 我？
我 跟 你 一起 去、跟 朋友 见见面。
词组：跟进、跟上、跟头

She is wearing a pair of high heels.
Why do you always follow me?
I will go with you, meet with friends.
Phrase: follow up, keep up, fall

227 月 yuè — Moon, month

月亮、月亮周期

Moon, lunar cycle

每月 二十五 号 发 工资。
岁月 静好。
今人 不见 古时 月，今 月 曾经 照 古人。
词组：正月、安全月、月牙

Salaries are paid on the 25th of every month.
Time flows peacefully.
People of today cannot see the moon of ancient times, yet the same moon once shone upon those of the past.
Phrase: first month, safe month, crescent moon

228 信 xìn — Trust, letter

诚实、消息、相信

Honesty, information, believe

诚信 才能 赢得 信赖。
有 航班 的 信息 吗？
可以 用 信用卡 付款 吗？
词组：信任、信号、信徒

Integrity is the key to earning trust.
Is there any flight information?
Can I pay by credit card?
Phrase: trust, signal, believer

229 山 shān Mountain

地表隆起的部分、高大、困难

传说中的 昆仑山 是 神仙 住 的 地方。
这里 山势 险峻，登山者 大多 在此 止步。
山泉 在 山间 奔流。
词组：高山、雪山、山区

The raised part of the earth's surface, tall, difficult

The legendary Kunlun Mountain is where the gods live.
The mountains here are steep and most climbers stop here.
The mountain springs flow in the mountains.
Phrases: high mountains, snow-capped mountains, mountainous areas

230 爱 ài Love

深挚的感情、喜好、珍惜

爱生活、爱笑、爱人 。
你 爱 干嘛 就 干嘛。
我们 只活 一次，应该 爱惜 光 阴。
词组：爱好、求爱、友爱

Deep affection, hobbies, cherish

Live, Laugh, Love.
Do whatever you love.
We only live once, so we should cherish time.
Phrases: hobbies, courtship, friendship

231 内 nèi Inside

内部

室内 比 室外 暖和 多了。
新的 内存 还在 做 内部 测 试。
年轻人 不喜欢 内卷。
词组：国内、内容、内脏

Internal

It is much warmer inside than outside.
The new memory chip is still undergoing internal testing.
Young people do not like involution.
Phrases: domestic, content, internal organs

232 龙 lóng Dragon

神话生物、代表权力和尊贵

中国人 自认 龙的 传人。
水 不在 深，有 龙 则 灵 。
恐龙 已经 灭绝了。
词组：龙卷风、龙舟

Mythical creature, representing power and dignity

Chinese people consider themselves descendants of the dragon.
Water doesn't need to be deep; it becomes magical if it has a dragon.
Dinosaurs are extinct.
Phrases: tornado, dragon boat

233 空 kōng — Empty

无物、没有结果

Nothing, no result

房间里空空的，没有家具。
你 有 空吗?
说的 都是 空话。
词组：天空、真空、空旷

The room is empty, no furniture.
Are you free?
Everything said is empty talk.
Phrase: sky, vacuum, open space

234 带 dài — Belt

条状物、附带、随身、率领

Strip, attached, carried, led

系好 安全带 。
你 带 钱包了吗?
没他 带头，我们 无法 走出
热带 雨林。
词组：领带、带劲、带领

Fasten your seat belt.
Did you bring your wallet?
Without him leading the way, we couldn't
get out of the rainforest.
Phrase: tie, exciting, lead

235 找 zhǎo — Search

搜寻、退还、引发

Search, return, cause

最近 在 找 工作。
这是 找 你的 零钱 。
答案 找到了吗?
词组：寻找、找对象、自找

I'm looking for a job recently.
This is your change.
Have you found the answer?
Phrases: search, find a partner, asking for
it

236 原 yuán — Original

初始的、本来的、广阔平地

Initial, original, vast plain

草原 尽头 有 一片 原生林。
原来 是 这样 。
愿 原力 与 你 同在!
词组：原罪、原点、原子

There is a virgin forest at the end of the
grassland.
So that's how it is.
May the Force be with you!
Phrases: sin, origin, atom

237 入 rù

Enter

进入空间、时间或状态

Entering into space, time or state

上海 是 长江 的 入海口。
宝宝 入睡 了。
准备 从 哪里 入手?
词组：入院、输入、收入

Shanghai is the estuary of the Yangtze River.
The baby fell asleep.
Where should we start preparing?
Phrase: admission to hospital, input, income

238 李 lǐ

Plum

一种果树、姓

A fruit tree, a surname

李子 味 酸甜 。
全球 有 超过 一亿 人 姓 李，
仅次于 王姓。

词组：桃李、行李、李四

Plums taste sweet and sour.
There are more than 100 million people with the surname Li in the world, second only to Wang.
Phrase: students, luggage, John Doe

239 连 lián

Connect

相接、持续、语气强调

Connected, continuous, emphasis tone

连日 风雪。
这起 案件 牵连 到 多人，接连 有人 被捕。
连 我 都 不 相信。

词组：连续、心连心、连长

Snowstorms for days.
This case involves many people, and people have been arrested one after another.
Even I don't believe it.
Phrase: continuous, heart to heart, company commander

240 吃 chī

Eat

摄入食物、消灭、承受外力和情感
小吃部 有 卖 吃的。
王军 吃了 一拳，大吃 一惊。
靠山 吃山。
词组：吃苦、吃亏、吃不准

Intake of food, elimination, withstand external forces and emotions
The snack bar sells food.
Wang Jun was shocked after taking a punch.
Live off the mountain if you live by it.
Phrases: suffer, suffer loss, be uncertain

241 场 chǎng — Field

活动地方和范围、量词

Place and scope of activities, quantifier

体育场 晚上 有 一场 篮球赛。
公共 场所，请 不要 大声 喧哗。
股票 市场 忽上 忽下。
词组：电场、现场、登场

There is a basketball game in the stadium tonight.
Please do not make loud noises in public places.
The stock market fluctuates up and down.
Phrase: electric field, scene, appearance

242 平 píng — Even

无凹凸、均等、安定

Smooth, even, stable

他 剃了 一个 小平头。
和平 来之 不易。
海平面 平均 高度 升高了。
词组：平手、平衡、平定

He shaved his head into a crew cut.
Peace is hard-won.
The average sea level has risen.
Phrase: draw, balance, put down

243 思 sī — Think

想、想念、想法

Think, miss, idea

夜深 人静 时 思绪 万千，非常 思念 你。
红豆 生 南国，此物 最 相思。
不好 意思。没关系，小 意思。
词组：思想、思索、构思

When the night is quiet, I have a lot of thoughts, and I miss you very much.
Red beans grow in the southern country; they are the most symbolic of longing.
I feel embarrassed. It's okay, it's nothing.
Phrase: thought, thinking, conceive

244 林 lín — Forest

大片草木、群体

Large area of grass and trees, groups

森林 大火 被 扑灭了。
独 木 不 成 林。
桂林 石林 是 独特 风景。
词组：竹林、林立、丛林

The forest fire was put out.
A lone tree does not make a forest.
Guilin Stone Forest is a unique landscape.
Phrase: bamboo forest, stand in great numbers, jungle

245 变 biàn — Change

转换、调整
Transformation, adjustment

变 是 正常 的，不变 是 不可思议 的。
Change is normal, not changing is unbelievable.

变天了，在下雨。要不要 变 个 时间 再 出去?
The weather has changed and it is raining. Do you want to go out at a different time?

时代 发生 巨变。
The times have changed dramatically.

词组：变化、变量、兵变
Phrase: change, variable, mutiny

246 使 shǐ — Cause

指令、引发、外交官
Instruct, induce, diplomat

使用 你们 的 产品 有 什么 好处?
What are the benefits of using your product?

大使 在 接待 外交 使团。
The ambassador is receiving a diplomatic mission.

女儿 是 个 小 天使。
The daughter is a little angel.

词组：指使、迫使、使命
Phrase: instruct, force, mission

247 由 yóu — Reason, from

起源与路径、听从
Origin and path, obey

你要 说出 理由，不是 借口。
You have to give reasons, not excuses.

货物 经由 海运 到达了 目的 地。
The goods arrived at the destination by sea.

相 由 心 生。
Appearance is born from the heart.

词组：必由、由我、自由
Phrases: must, by me, free

248 受 shòu — Receive

接纳、被动承受
Accept, passively bear

让 您 受累 了。
Sorry for the trouble.

受灾 的 民众 接受了 捐赠。
The people affected by the disaster accepted the donation.

你 倒是 知道 享受。
You know how to enjoy it.

词组：感受、好受、受骗
Phrases: feel, feel good, be deceived

249 亲 qīn — Relatives

血缘、肢体亲近、感情好、自己

Blood relationship, physical closeness, good feelings, oneself

他的 双亲 都 健在。
家乡 的 一切 都 使我 感到 亲切。
你还 写 亲笔 信?
词组: 亲人、亲吻、亲密

Both of his parents are alive.
Everything about my hometown feels so familiar and dear to me.
Do you still write handwritten letters?
Phrases: relatives, kiss, close

250 命 mìng — Life

生命本体、天命、指示

Life essence, destiny, instructions

野草 具有 顽强 的 生命力。
有人 相信 人的 命运 是 命中注定的。
妈妈的 命令 必须 服从。
词组: 任命、救民、革命

Wild grass has a tenacious vitality.
Some people believe that people's fate is predetermined.
Mother's orders must be obeyed.
Phrase: appointment, salvation, revolution

251 目 mù — Eye

眼睛、观察、条目

Eyes, observation, classification

她 眉清 目秀。
千万 不要 盲目 投资。
这是 演出的 节目单。
词组: 目的、科目、项目

She has a pretty face.
Don't invest blindly.
This is the program for the performance.
Phrase: purpose, subject, project

252 强 qiáng — Strong

健壮 、程度高 、使用强力

Strong, high level, use of force

多锻炼,身体 才能 强壮。
面对 强手 , 我们 不能 胆怯。
自己 不 喜欢的 事情,不要 强加 于人。
词组: 富强、强健、强加

Exercise more to make your body strong.
We must not be timid in the face of strong opponents.
Don't impose on others what you don't like.
Phrase: rich, strong, impose

253 男 nán — Men

阳性的人、儿子

Human male, a son

他 是 家中 唯一的 男孩。
班上 男生 比 女生 多。
前 男友 是 个 渣男。
词组：男童、俊男、男方

He is the only boy in the family.
There are more boys than girls in the class.
The ex-boyfriend is a jerk.
Phrase: boy, handsome man, man's side

254 任 rèn — Appoint

职务委派、承担、相信、听凭

Delegation, undertaking, trust, and leave to others

经理 是 新 任命 的。
警察 有 责任 依法 行事。
今天的 任务 很快 就 完成了。
词组：任性、任免、升任

The manager is newly appointed.
The police have the responsibility to act in accordance with the law.
Today's task was quickly completed.
Phrase: capricious, appointment and removal, promotion

255 该 gāi — Should

应当、必须、代替前文、表示推测或感叹

Should, must, replace the previous text, express speculation or exclamation

你 生病了，该 好好 休息。
他 违反了 规定，该行为 必须 受到 处罚。
这么 做，该 有 多 危险 啊!
词组：应该、该死、活该

You are sick, you should rest well.
He violated the rules and must be punished for this behavior.
How dangerous it is for you to do this!
Phrases: should, damn, deserve it

256 路 lù — Road

通道、途径

Passage, way

南京路 与 中山路 交汇处。
莫愁 前路 无 知己。
条条 大路 通 罗马。
词组：路边、走路、引路

The intersection of Nanjing Road and Zhongshan Road.
Don't worry that there are no friends ahead on your journey.
All roads lead to Rome.
Phrase: roadside, walk, guide like.

257 车 chē — Vehicle

有轮子的交通工具、机械装置　A vehicle or mechanical device

汽车 被 吊车 吊了 起来。
列车 经过 了 火车站，没停。
驱车 登 古原。
词组：车床、车次、房车

The car was lifted by a crane.
The train passed the railway station without stopping.
Driving up to the ancient plain.
Phrase: lathe, train number, RV

258 今 jīn — Now

当前的时间、当代　Current time, contemporary

今天 运气 很好。
古今 同 日月。
今生 今世 不能 将你 相忘。
词组：当今、今晚、至今

I have good luck today.
The past and present share the same sun and moon.
In this life and this world, I cannot forget you.
Phrases: today, tonight, till now

259 海 hǎi — Sea

海洋、数量极多　Ocean, a large number

我们 到 海边 去 看海。
街上 人山 人海。
他 是 海外 华侨。
词组：海鲜、海关、海拔

We went to the beach to see the sea.
The streets were crowded with people.
He is an overseas Chinese.
Phrase: seafood, customs, altitude

260 加 jiā — Increase

增多、添加、给与　Increase, add, give

加倍 是 一个数 加上 自己。
欢迎 你 加入 我们 部门。
他们 加工厂 增加 了 加班费。
词组：加法、加紧、附加

Double is a number plus itself.
Welcome to join our department.
Their processing plant has added overtime pay.
Phrases: addition, speed up, additional

261 远 yuǎn

Distant

距离长、时间长

Long distance, long time

隔着山沟，看上去不远，走起来远。
Across the ravine, it looks not far, but it is far away.

旧事 如 天 远。
The past is as far away as the sky.

远景 还是 很 美妙的。
The distant view is still very beautiful.

词组：远古、远门、永远
Phrases: ancient times, far away, forever

262 活 huó

Live

生存、使生存、生动的、工作

Survive, make survive, lively, work

活着 就是 成功。
Being alive is success.

他 干活 是 为了 养活 全家。
He works to support his family.

大 活人，脑子 灵活点。
A living person should be more flexible in his mind.

词组：活动、活水、生活
Phrases: activity, running water, life

263 特 tè

Special

超出一般、专门

Beyond the ordinary, special

看不出 他 有 什么 特别。
I can't see what's special about him.

这个 特产 是 特地 给 你 买 的。
This specialty is bought especially for you.

深圳 特区 有 特殊的 经济 政策。
The Shenzhen Special Economic Zone has special economic policies.

词组：特色、特权、特性
Phrase: characteristics, privileges, features

264 解 jiě

Untie

分开、消除、说明

Separate, eliminate, explain

热了 就把 衣服 解开。
When it gets hot, just loosen your clothes.

我 也是 一知 半解。
I also only have a partial understanding.

这个 方程 无解。
This equation has no solution.

词组：解气、溶解、解手
Phrases: relieve anger, dissolve, relieve oneself

265 电 diàn — Electricity

闪电、与电相关
Lightning, electricity-related

古人 以为 雷鸣 闪电 是 天神 发怒。
The ancients believed that thunder and lightning were the wrath of the gods.

电闸 跳了。
The switch tripped.

光电 效应 将 光能 转换成 电能。
The photoelectric effect converts light energy into electrical energy.

词组：电压、电筒、电子
Phrases: voltage, flashlight, electron

266 世 shì — Generation

一代、时代、人类活动空间
Generation, era, space for human activities

赵阳 家 四世 同堂。
Zhao Yang's family has four generations living together.

世界 进入 了 二十一 世纪。
The world has entered the 21st century.

佛教 中的 世 是 轮回、世俗 的 意思。
The word "shi" in Buddhism means reincarnation and secular life.

词组：世间、永世、逝世
Phrase: worldly, forever, death

267 性 xìng — Nature

本质、性格、性别
Nature, character, gender

人之初，性本善。
At the beginning, humans are inherently good in nature.

他 性格 阳光。
He has a sunny personality.

男性 女性 性别 不同。
Men and women have different genders.

词组：性能、性情、磁性
Phrase: property, temperament, magnetism

268 表 biǎo — Surface

外部表面、表达、手表、分类
External surface, expression, watch, classification

他 表演 时 的 表情 非常 夸张。
His expression during the performance was very exaggerated.

地表 水 枯竭了。
The surface water dried up.

表扬 他 是 因为 他 表现 好。
He was praised for his good performance.

词组：外表、表格、表明
Phrase: appearance, form, indicate

269 许 xǔ

Promise

同意、多、可能

Agree, many, maybe

你 必须 兑现 你的 许诺。
许多人 都说 这个 软件 不需要 许可证。
也许 你 说的 是 对的。
词组：许久、许配、准许

You must keep your promise.
Many people say that this software does not need a license.
Maybe you are right.
Phrases: for a long time, betrothed, allow

270 它 tā

It

指代人以外的事物

Refers to things other than people

猫 很 可爱，但 它 会 掉毛。
它们 是 珍稀 动物。
除了 它们，其它 的 花 在 雪中 是 不能 盛开 的。
词组：它山之石

Cats are cute, but they shed.
They are rare animals.
Besides them, other flowers cannot bloom in the snow.
Phrase: stone from another mountain

271 立 lì

Stand

站在地面、制定、即刻

Stand on the ground, formulate, immediately

人 是 唯一 直立 行走 的 动物。
整改 必须 立刻 执行，要 达到 立竿 见影 的 效果。
词组：独立、孤立、立正

Humans are the only animals that walk upright.
The rectification must be carried out immediately to achieve instant and noticeable results.
Phrase: independent, isolated, stand at attention

272 黑 hēi

Black

暗的颜色和光线、掩蔽的、恶毒

Dark colors and light, concealed, malicious

天 黑 了，房间 里 黑洞洞 的。
他 自诩 心肠 黑，是 黑道 上 的人。
词组：乌黑、抹黑、黑洞

It was dark, and the room was pitch black.
He prides himself on having a dark heart and claims to be part of the underworld.
Phrase: black, smear, black hole

273 金 jīn — Gold

金属、化学元素、金钱

Metal, chemical element, money

金是一种非常稳定的金属。
黄金历史上一直是财富和权力的象征。
千金散尽还复来。
词组：金黄、合金、现金

Gold is a very stable metal.
Gold has been a symbol of wealth and power throughout history.
A thousand pieces of gold spent will return again.
Phrases: golden, alloy, cash

274 红 hóng — Red

红颜色

Red color

中国红是一种深红色调的颜色。红色被认为是帝王色彩和尊贵身份的象征。在民间，红色又是吉祥的象征。
词组：红包、分红、走红

China Red is a shade of deep red. Red is considered a symbol of imperial grandeur and noble status. Among the people, red is also regarded as a symbol of good fortune.
Phrases: red envelope, dividend, becoming popular

275 花 huā — Flower

花朵、像花的东西

Flowers, things that look like flowers

花园里盛开各种鲜花。
桃花依旧笑春风。
花猫好奇地看着雪花纷飞。
词组：花菜、棉花、花样

Various flowers are blooming in the garden.
The peach blossoms are still smiling in the spring breeze.
The tabby cat is curiously watching the snowflakes flying.
Phrase: cauliflower, cotton, pattern

276 转 (1)zhuàn (2)zhuǎn — Turn

(1) 车轮转动 (2) 改变方向或状态、迁移
地球绕太阳旋转[1]。
你转[2]头就能看见。
请转[2]达我的问候。
词组：自转[1]、转[2]机、转[2]运

(1) Wheel turns (2) Change direction or state, migrate
The earth rotates around the sun.
You can see it if you turn your head.
Please convey my regards.
Phrase: rotation, turning point, transport

277 总 zǒng　Total

聚合、全部、统领、经常　Aggregate, all, command, often

从 1 加 到 5 总和 是 15。　The sum of 1 to 5 is 15.
总部 对 我们 的 工作 总体上 是 满意的。　The headquarters is generally satisfied with our work.
你 不能 总是 迟到。　You can't always be late.
词组：总统、总结、总计　Phrases: president, summary, total

278 算 suàn　Count

计数、推测、有效、总结　Count, guess, effective, summarize

你 算 一下 这个 月 我们 花了 多少 钱。　Calculate how much we spent this month.
我 掐指 一算，你 今年 有 好 运。　I counted with my fingers, it seems you'll have good fortune this year.
算了，算了，就算 我 倒霉。　Ah, forget it, forget it, let's just say it's my bad luck.
词组：算术、算法、计算　Phrases: arithmetic, algorithm, calculation

279 城 chéng　City

城墙、城市、功能区域　Wall, city, functional area

长城 是 军事 防御 工事。　Great Wall is a military fortification.
南京 城 古时 又 叫 石头城。　Nanjing City was also called Stone City in ancient times.
横店 是 个 影视城。　Hengdian is a film and television city.
词组：城门、城乡、省城　Phrases: city gate, urban and rural areas, provincial capital

280 队 duì　Team

队伍、排列、组织　Team, arrangement, organization

部队 列队 出发。　The troops lined up to set out.
我们 球队 一队 新手，不成 队形。　Our team is a group of rookies, and they couldn't form a formation.
销售 团队 业绩 很好。　The sales team performed very well.
词组：队长、军队、梯队　Phrases: captain, army, echelon

281 孩 hái

儿童、子女

你有几个孩子?
他有点孩子气。
在家生孩子养孩子也不错。
词组:小孩、熊孩子、乖孩子

Child

Children, offspring

How many children do you have?
He is a bit childish.
Having and raising children at home isn't bad either.
Phrase: child, naughty child, good child

---

282 反 fǎn

翻转、对立、回击、违背

这盘棋我本是准赢的,没想到被反杀了。
不要我说什么你都反对。
违反自然规律是要受惩罚的。
词组:反应、相反、反射

Reverse

Reverse, oppose, fight back, violate

I was sure to win this game, but I was defeated unexpectedly.
Don't oppose everything I say.
Violating the laws of nature will be punished.
Phrase: reaction, opposite, reflection

---

283 工 gōng

拿工具劳动、劳动者、精细

工厂有一千多工人。
工程师认为工程需要三十天。
他写的字非常工整。
词组:工业、完工、工作

Labor

To work with tools, laborer, fine

The factory has more than a thousand workers.
The engineer thinks the project will take thirty days.
He writes very neatly.
Phrase: industry, completion, work

---

284 始 shǐ

生命诞生之初、开始、根源

他从始至终都没有休息。
秦始皇统一了中国。
千里之行,始于足下。
词组:创始、原始

Begin

The beginning of life, start, origin

He never rested from beginning to end.
Qin Shi Huang unified China.
A journey of a thousand miles begins with a single step.
Phrases: founding, original

285 满 mǎn　Full

水装满容器、充实、全部　Water fills the container, fills up, all

得了 满分，满意吧？
是的，满心 欢喜。
要 不 小心，满盘 皆输。
词组：圆满、美满、满口

You got full marks, are you satisfied?
Yes, I am very happy.
If you are not careful, you will lose everything.
Phrase: perfect, happy, mouthful

286 新 xīn　New

初始、改变旧状、最近　Initial, change from the old state, recent

新年 新 气象。
你家 房子 翻新了？
新郎 和 新娘 在 新房 里面。
词组：新闻、新鲜、新近

New Year, new atmosphere.
Has your house been renovated?
The bride and groom are in the bridal chamber.
Phrase: news, fresh, recent

287 兵 bīng　Solider

武器、战士、军队、军事　Weapons, soldiers, army, military

兵工厂 建在 山里。
中国 的 士兵 绝大多数 为 志愿兵。
养兵 千日，用兵 一时。
词组：交兵、兵器、兵法

Arsenals are built in the mountains.
The vast majority of Chinese soldiers are volunteers.
Raise soldiers for a thousand days, use them for one moment.
Phrase: fighting, weapons, military tactics

288 物 wù　Thing

万物、内容　All things, content

博物馆 里 藏有 各种 生物 样本。
四川 物产 丰富。
任何 事物 都 不是 一成不变 的。
词组：物理、人物、实物

The museum contains various biological specimens.
Sichuan is rich in natural resources.
Nothing remains unchanged.
Phrases: physics, notable individual, tangible objects

289 离 lí

Depart

分开、相隔、不合

Separate, apart, incompatible

你什么时候 离开 家的?
火星 是 离 地球 最近的 行星。
人有 悲欢 离合。
词组：离职、隔离、离心机

When did you leave home?
Mars is the closest planet to the Earth.
People experience joys and sorrows, separations and reunions.
Phrase: resign, isolate, centrifuge

290 非 fēi

Not

否定、错误、不属于

Negative, wrong, not belonging

有人 的地方 就有 是非。
这是 样品，非 卖品。
非 你 不嫁。非 你 不娶。
词组：非常、非凡、非议

Where there are people, there is gossip.
This is a sample, not for sale.
I will not marry anyone but you.
Phrase: very, extraordinary, criticism

291 虽 suī

Although

表示让步的连词、强调对比或例外

Conjunctions that indicate concession, emphasize contrast or exception

虽 天气 很糟，他 坚持 开车。
虽 败 犹 荣。
牡丹 虽好，也要 绿叶 扶持。
词组：虽然、虽说、虽有

Although the weather was bad, he insisted on driving.
Defeated but still glorious.
Although the peony is beautiful, it still needs the support of green leaves.
Phrase: although, although, although there is

292 云 yún

Cloud

云朵、众多、比喻飘渺

Clouds, numerous, metaphor for being ethereal

白云 生处 有 人家。
广交会 商家 云集。
世间 万物，犹如 过眼 云烟。
词组：云雾、云霄、云计算

Where the white clouds arise, there are homes.
The Canton Fair is crowded with merchants.
All things in the world are like fleeting clouds before the eyes.
Phrases: clouds, high clouds, cloud computing

293 似 sì — Resemble

相像、好像

Similar, like

类似 的 题目 我 见过。
I have seen similar question.

天上 布满 黑云，似乎要 下雨了。
The sky is full of dark clouds, and it seems that it is going to rain.

时光 似 箭。
Time flies like an arrow.

词组：相似、胜似、貌似
Phrases: similar, better than, seemingly

294 万 wàn — Ten thousand

十个一千、极多、很

Ten thousand, a lot, very

祝 万事 如意!
I wish you all the best!

万分 感谢!
Thank you very much!

万幸，事故中 没有 人 受伤。
Fortunately, no one was injured in the accident.

词组：万维网、万全、万众
Phrases: World Wide Web, perfect, thousands of people

295 至 zhì — Arrive

到达、极点、最

To reach, the apex, the highest

他 至死 都 没有 明白 是 谁 伤害 了 他。
Until his death, he never understood who had hurt him.

事 已至此，就 不要 再 折腾了。
Since things have come to this, stop tossing and turning over it.

至亲 好友 都 参加了 婚礼。
All the close relatives and friends attended the wedding.

词组：直至、至高、冬至
Phrases: until, the highest, the winter solstice

296 干 (1)gān (2) gàn — Dry, work

(1) 无水、涉及 (2) 主体、从事

(1) no water, involving (2) subject, engaged in

天气 干¹旱，河水 都 干¹了。
The weather is dry, the river water has dried up.

你 不要 干¹涉，与 你 何 干¹?
Don't interfere, what does it have to do with you?

干²部 带头 苦干² 实干²。
The cadres took the lead in hard work.

词组：干¹燥、干¹杯、干²线
Phrases: dry, cheers, main line

297 通 tōng

无阻、全面、交流、透彻

三条 高速 通过 这里。
他 通晓 世界 历史。
通知 准时 送到 了。
词组：通畅、通才、通讯

Pass

Unobstructed, comprehensive, communication, thorough

Three highways pass through here.
He knows world history.
The notice was delivered on time.
Phrases: smooth, generalist, communication

298 认 rèn

辨别、接受、态度

你 认识 黄小明 吗？
错了 就要 认错。
他 工作 踏实 认真。
词组：确认、承认、公认

Recognize

Identify, accept, attitude

Do you know Huang Xiaoming?
If you are wrong, you must admit it.
He works diligently and conscientiously.
Phrase: confirm, admit, recognized

299 失 shī

丢失、失误、缺失、错过

钱包 丢失了？去 问 一下 失物
招领。
可以 失败，不可以 失志；可以
失望，不可以 绝望。
错失 相会 的 机会，心中 不免
失落。
词组：失态、失眠、失意

Lose

Lost, mistake, missing, missed

Lost your wallet? Check lost and found.
You can fail, but you can't lose your will; you can be disappointed, but you can't despair.
Missed the opportunity to meet, and you can't help feeling lost.
Phrase: Lost your temper, insomnia, frustration

300 火 huǒ

火焰、燃烧、激烈、热度

房子 被 火 烧掉 了。
他 脾气 火爆。
生意 很 红火。
词组：火灾、救火、妒火

Fire

Flame, burning, intense, popularity

The house was burned down by fire.
He has a hot temper.
Business is booming.
Phrase: fire, firefighting, jealousy

谢 xiè

感谢、结束、拒绝

谢谢! 非常 感谢!
花 谢了。
我 谢绝了 邀请。
词组：谢罪、谢客、谢世

Thank

Thank you, end, refuse

Thank you! Thank you very much!
The flowers have withered.
I declined the invitation.
Phrases: apologize, decline visitors, pass away

校 xiào

教育机构、军衔

学校 的 学生 穿着 校服。
校园 里 到处 是 回来 参加 校庆 的 校友。
上校 是 军校 毕业生。
词组：技校、校长、校外

School

Educational institution, military rank

Students in the school wear uniforms.
The campus is full of alumni who have returned to attend the school anniversary.
Colonel is a graduate of a military academy.
Phrase: technical school, principal, off-campus

请 qǐng

要求、表达敬意、强调意愿

请 坐。
请问 到北海 怎么 走?
请勿 吸烟。
词组：请示、请假、请求

Ask

Request, show respect, emphasize willingness
Please take a seat.
Excuse me, how do I get to Beihai?
Please do not smoke.
Phrase: ask for instructions, ask for leave, request

钱 qián

货币、财富

猪肉 多少 钱 一斤?
他 即会 挣钱，又会 存钱。
有钱 能 使 鬼 推磨。
词组：金钱、零钱、花钱

Money

Currency, wealth

How much does pork cost per pound?
He knows how to make money and save money.
Money can make the devil turn the millstone.
Phrase: money, change, spend money

饭 fàn

煮熟的主食、进食、餐次

煮饭时一杯米加 1.2 杯水，饭
更软。
小东，妈妈 喊 你 回家 吃饭。
饭堂 什么 时候 开饭？
词组：饭店、讨饭、饭桶

Meal

Cooked staple food, eating, meal times

When cooking rice, add 1.2 cups of
water to one cup of rice to make the rice
softer.
Xiao Dong, your mother is calling you to
come home for dinner.
When does the canteen open for dinner?
Phrase: restaurant, begging, fool

店 diàn

商业场所

小店 堆满 了 各种 商品。
饭店 在 药店 隔壁。
书店 里 的 店员 帮我 找到了
我 要的 书。
词组：商店、旅店、门店

Shop

Commercial places

The small shop is filled with all kinds of
goods.
The restaurant is next to the drugstore.
The clerk in the bookstore helped me
find the book I wanted.
Phrases: shop, hotel, store

喝 (1)hē (2) hè

(1) 吞咽液体 (2) 大喊

请 喝 茶。
他 喝 醉了。
观众 发出 阵阵 喝彩 声。
词组：喝下、吆喝、喝止

Drink, shout

(1) Swallow liquid (2) Shout

Have some tea, please.
He is drunk.
The audience burst into waves of cheers.
Phrases: drink, shout, stop

跑 pǎo

快速移动、逃避

我们 来 赛跑。
警察 已经 盯上 你，别想 跑
掉。
我们 是 领跑者。
词组：起跑、长跑

Run

Move quickly, escape

Let's race.
The police are already watching you;
don't think you can run away.
We are the front runners.
Phrases: start, long-distance running

买 mǎi 卖 mài — Buy, sell

以货币换取 — Exchange money for

买点 牛奶。	Buy some milk.
做的 都是 小买卖。	It's all small-scale businesses.
寸 金 难 买 寸 光阴。	An inch of gold cannot buy an inch of time.
词组：收买、买单、赎买	Phrase: buy, pay, redeem

市 shì — Market

交易场所、城市 — Trading place, city

菜 市场 有 各种 蔬菜。	The vegetable market has all kinds of vegetables.
西安 市 是 一座 历史 名城。	Xi'an is a famous historical city.
股市 今天 休市。	The stock market is closed today.
词组：市区、市场、市长	Phrases: urban area, market, mayor

爸 bà 妈 mā — Father, mother

父亲、母亲 — Father, Mother

爸爸 和 妈妈 从不 吵架。	Dad and Mom never quarrel.
姑妈 是 爸爸的 姐妹。	Aunt is Dad's sister.
词组：阿爸、老妈、姨妈	Phrase: Dad, Mom, aunt

网 wǎng — Web

捕猎工具、抽象结构、捕捉 — Hunting tools, abstract structures, capture

渔民 用 渔网 捕鱼。	Fishermen use fishing nets to catch fish.
我们 已经 离不开 互联网。	We can no longer live without the internet.
公司 有 很多 网点。	The company has many outlets.
词组：电网、关系网、网红	Phrase: power grid, relationship network, internet celebrity

阅读练习

短诗

远看山有色，
近听水无声。
春去花还在，
人来鸟不惊。

作者：王维

一去二三里，
烟村四五家。
亭台六七座，
八九十枝花。

作者：宋邵雍

好雨知时节，
当春乃发生。
随风潜入夜，
润物细无声。

作者：杜甫

白日依山尽，
黄河入海流。
欲穷千里目，
更上一层楼。

作者：王之涣

你，
一会看我，
一会看云。
我觉得，
你看我时很远，
你看云时很近。

作者：顾城

Short poem

近 close
春 spring
鸟 bird 惊 panic

烟 smoke 村 village 五 five
亭台 pavilion 六 six 七 seven 座
quantifier 八 eight 九 nine 枝 quantifier

雨 rain 节 season
乃 only
随 follow 潜 hidden 夜 night
润 moisten 细 thin

依 lean 尽 end
黄河 Yellow river 流 flow
欲 wish 穷 exhaust 千 thousand
层 layer 楼 building

黑夜给了我黑色的眼睛
我却用它寻找光明

作者：顾城

陌生人，我也为你祝福	陌生 stranger 祝福 bless
愿你有一个灿烂的前程	愿 wish 灿烂 splendid 程 journey
愿你有情人终成眷属	终 finally 眷属 family
愿你在尘世获得幸福	尘世 this world 获 capture 幸福
我只愿面朝大海，春暖花开	happiness 朝 towards 暖 warm

作者：海子

悄悄的我走了，	悄 quite
正如我悄悄的来；	
我挥一挥衣袖，	挥 wave 衣袖 sleeves
不带走一片云彩。	片 quantifier 云彩 cloud

作者：徐志摩

小笑话 | # Humor

A：你可知道，人类先有男人还是先有女人？	类 kind
B：先有男人。	
A：根据什么？	根据 according to
B：这都不知道，我们的男人称先生，不就是一个铁证吗？	铁证 irrefutable evidence

有一次我爸妈吵架，我妈很生气地说了句："你给我滚出去。"	吵架 quarrel
我爸气得说了句："我给你滚出去！"	滚 roll, get out of here

钱不是问题，问题是没钱。	问题 problem

匆匆

燕子去了，有再来的时候；杨柳枯了，有再青的时候；桃花谢了，有再开的时候。但是，聪明的，你告诉我，我们的日子为什么一去不复返呢？——是有人偷了他们罢：那是谁？又藏在何处呢？是他们自己逃走了：现在又到了哪里呢？我不知道他们给了我多少日子；但我的手确乎是渐渐空虚了。在默默里算着，八千多日子已经从我手中溜去；象针尖上一滴水滴在大海里，我的日子滴在时间的流里，没有声音也没有影子。我不禁头涔涔而泪潸潸了。

去的尽管去了，来的尽管来着，去来的中间，又怎样的匆匆呢？早上我起来的时候，小屋里射进两三方斜斜的太阳。太阳他有脚啊，轻轻悄悄地挪移了；我也茫茫然跟着旋转。于是——洗手的时候，日子从水盆里过去；吃饭的时候，日子从饭碗里过去；默默时，便从凝然的双眼前过去。我觉察他去的匆匆了，伸出手遮挽时，他又从遮挽着的手边过去，天黑时，我躺在床上，他便伶伶俐俐地从我身边跨过，从我脚边飞去了。等我睁开眼和太阳再见，这算又溜走了一日。我掩着面叹息。但是新来的日子的影儿又开始在叹息里闪过了。

在逃去如飞的日子里，在千门万户的世界里的我能做些什么呢？只有徘徊罢了，只有匆匆罢了；在八千多日的匆匆里，除徘徊外，又剩些什么呢？过去的日子如轻烟却被微风吹散了，如薄

燕 swallow 时候 time 杨柳 willow
青 green 桃 peach
聪 smart
告诉 tell
复返 return 偷 steal
罢 吧 谁 who
藏 hide 逃 escape

确乎 indeed 渐 gradually 虚 empty
默 silent
溜 slip 象 like 针尖 needle point
滴 drop
流 flow 音 sound
影 shadow 不禁 can't help 涔 watery
潸 shed tears

尽管 although

早 morning 屋 room 射 shoot
斜 incline 太阳 sun 脚 foot
挪移 move 茫 vague
旋 spin 洗 wash
盆 pot
碗 bowl
凝 freeze 双 double
觉察 aware 伸 stretch 遮挽 hold back
躺 lie 床 bed
伶俐 clever 跨 step astride
睁 open eyes
掩 cover
叹息 sigh
闪 flash

户 household 世界 world
徘徊 wander

剩 left
微 tiny 吹散 blow away 薄雾 mist

雾，被初阳蒸融了；我留着些什么痕迹呢？我何曾留着象游丝样的痕迹呢？我赤裸裸来到这世界，转眼间也将赤裸裸地回去罢？但不能平的，为什么偏要白白走这一遭啊？

你聪明的，告诉我，我们的日子为什么一去不复返呢？

作者：朱自清

初阳 morning sun 蒸融 evaporate 留 keep 痕迹 trace 何曾 ever 游丝 gossamer 赤裸 naked

偏要 have to 一遭 once

小笑话

有个人第一次在集市上卖花生，不好意思叫卖，正好边上有一个人高声叫喊："卖花生。"于是他跟着喊道："我也是。"

花生 peanut 集市 country fair
喊 shout

一次小明放学回到家后对他妈妈说："妈妈，我是我们班力气最大的，我以后一定能成为大力士。"
妈妈说："你哪来的自信？"
小明说："老师给的啊！我们老师总是说，我一人拖了我们全班的后腿呢！"

班 class
士 warrior

拖 drag 腿 leg
拖后腿 hinder

全家人开着新买的车出外游玩。突然，车不动了，一家人顶着烈日用力推车，推了两个小时。
爸爸站住了："我现在总算明白那卖车人的话是什么意思了。"
妈妈一边擦汗一边问："他说什么来着？"
"他说这车非常省油。"

游玩 play 突然 suddenly 顶 top 烈日 scorching sun 推 push 站 stand

擦汗 wipe sweat
省油 fuel efficient

你爸姓张，你姓什么？

姓 last name

海上日出

为了看日出，我常常早起。那时天还没有大亮，周围非常冷清，船上只有机器的响声。

天空还是一片浅蓝，颜色很浅。转眼间天边出现了一道红霞，慢慢地在扩大它的范围，加强它的亮光。我知道太阳要从天边升起来了，便目不转睛地望着那里。

果然过了一会儿，在那个地方出现了太阳的小半边脸，红是真红，却没有亮光。这个太阳好像负着重荷似的一步一步，慢慢地努力上升，到了最后，终于冲破了云霞，完全跳出了海面，颜色红的非常可爱。一霎那间，这个深红的圆东西，忽然间发出了夺目的亮光，射得人眼睛发痛，它旁边的云片也忽然有了光彩。

有时太阳走进了云堆中，它的光线却从云里射下来，直射到水面上。这时候要分辨出哪里是水，哪里是天，倒也不容易，因为我就只看见一片灿烂的亮光。

有时天边有黑云，而且云片很厚，太阳出来，人眼还看不见。然而太阳在黑云里放射的光芒，透过黑云的重围，替黑云镶了一道发光的金边。后来太阳才慢慢地冲出重围，出现在天空，甚至把黑云也染成了紫色或者红色。这时候发亮的不仅是太阳、云和海水，连我自己也成了明亮的了。

作者：巴金

亮 bright 周围 surrounding 冷清 deserted 船 boat 机器 machine 响 sound

浅蓝 light blue 颜色 color
转眼间 blink of an eye 红霞 red clouds 慢 slowly 扩 expand 范围 range 升 rise

果然 sure enough
半 half

负 bear 重荷 weight 步 step
努力 strive
终于 finally 冲破 break through 跳 jump 霎那 instantly
深 deep 圆 round 忽然 suddenly 夺 目 eye-catching 痛 pain
旁 side 彩 color

堆 heap

分辨 distinguish
容易 easy

厚 thick
光芒 light
透 through 围 surround 替 for 镶 inlay

染 dye 紫 purple
仅 only

暗淡蓝点

从遥远的太空回望地球，地球只是一个暗淡的蓝色光点，似乎微不足道。但对我们来说，这里不可小看。请你再次凝望那个光点。它就在那里。它就是家乡。它就是我们。你所爱的每一个人，你认识的每一个人，你听说过的每一个人，曾经存在的每一个人，都在它上面度过一生。我们所有的悲欢离合，各种宗教和学派，每一位猎人与农民，每一位英雄与懦夫，每一个文明的缔造者与毁灭者，每一位国王与平民，每一对相爱的人，每一位母亲与父亲，满怀希望的孩子，发明家与探险家，每一位"君子"，贪官，"超级明星"，"至高领袖"，人类历史上的每一位圣人与罪人——都生活在这粒悬浮于阳光下的微尘之上。

地球的舞台在浩瀚的宇宙中是那么渺小。想想那些将军和国王，曾让多少人血流成河，仅仅为了荣耀与凯旋，仅仅为了成为这粒微尘上某个碎片的短暂主宰。想想这像素一角的人们，对另一角落几乎无以区分的人们，施加的无穷暴行。他们的误解何其经常，多么渴望自相残杀，仇恨又是何等狂热。

我们的傲慢，我们的自命不凡，我们自命天之骄子的妄想，都被这粒苍白的光点粉碎。我们的星球不过是宏大宇宙黑洞中的一粒孤独的尘埃。在我们的模糊的视野里，在浩瀚的宇宙中，看不见任何外来的救世主会来拯救我们。

Pale Blue Dot

遥远 distant 球 ball
暗淡 pale 蓝 blue 似乎 seem
微不足道 insignificant
凝望 stare
乡 township

认识 know
曾经 once 存在 exist
度 spend 悲欢离合 joys and sorrows
各种 all kind 宗教 religion 派 group
猎 hunt 农民 farmer
英雄 hero 懦夫 coward 缔造 create
毁灭 destroy
母 mother 父 father 满怀希望
hopeful 发明 invent 探险 adventure
君子 gentlemen 贪官 corrupt
officials 超级明星 superstar 领袖
leader 类 kind 历史 history 圣 saint
罪 crime 粒 grain 悬浮 float 微 tiny
尘 dust

舞台 stage 浩瀚 vast 宇宙 universe
渺 insignificant 将军 general
血 blood 流 flow 河 river 仅 only 荣
耀 glory 凯旋 triumph
某 certain 碎片 fragment 短暂
temporary 主宰 master 像素 pixel
角落 corner 几乎 almost 施加
impose 无穷暴行 endless cruelties
误解 misunderstandings 残 brutal 仇
恨 hatred 何等 how 狂热 fervent

傲慢 arrogant 凡 ordinary 骄 proud
妄 delusion
苍 gray 粉碎 smash 宏 spacious
洞 cave 孤独 lonely 尘埃 dust
模糊 vague 视野 vision

拯救 save

地球是目前已知唯一孕育生命的星球。至少在可预见的未来，人类无处迁徙。看望或许可行，安家还无可能。无论你是否情愿，今天的地球仍是我们唯一的立足之地。

唯一 only 孕育 give birth to
预 advance 未 not yet
迁徙 migrate
无论 regardless
足 foot

有人说，天文学使人谦卑还能修身养性。这张微小世界的远景，最生动地展示了人类自负的荒谬。在我看来，它更强调了我们的使命，友爱友好，珍爱与守望这粒淡蓝的微尘——我们唯一的家园。

谦卑 humble
修身养性 cultivate your character
景 view 展示 demonstrate 自负 conceit 荒谬 folly 强调 underscore
珍 treasure 守 guard
园 garden

译自 *Carl Sagan* 《Pale Blue Dot》

袋鼠与笼子

Kangaroo and cage

一天动物管理员们发现袋鼠从笼子里跑了出来，一致认为是笼子的高度过低。所以他们将笼子的高度由原来的十公尺加高到二十公尺。结果他们发现袋鼠还是跑到外面来，所以他们又决定加高到三十公尺。

动物管理员 animal keeper
袋鼠 kangaroo 笼 cage 高度 height 一致 unanimous 低 low 公尺 meter 结果 result

没想到第二天又看到袋鼠全跑到外面。于是管理员们大为紧张，决定一不做二不休，将笼子的高度加高到一百公尺。

紧张 nervous 决定 decide 休 rest

一天，长颈鹿和几只袋鼠们在闲聊。

长颈鹿 giraffe 闲聊 chat

"你们看，这些人会不会再继续加高你们的笼子？"长颈鹿问。

继续 continue

"很难说。"袋鼠说，"如果他们再继续忘记关门的话！"

忘记 forget

选自《伊索寓言》

301–600

301–400

哥 gē	哥哥 brother			象 xiàng	大象 elephant	
士 shì	战士 warrior			容 róng	类容 content	
五 wǔ	第五 number five			怪 guài	奇怪 strange	
惊 jīng	吃惊 shock			传 chuán	传递 pass	
魔 mó	魔鬼 devil			钱 qián	钱 money	
竟 jìng	竟然 unexpectedly			提 tí	提醒 prompt	
姐 jiě	姐姐 elder sister			言 yán	言语 words	
乎 hū	几乎 almost			随 suí	跟随 follow	
剑 jiàn	剑 sword			每 měi	每次 every	
往 wǎng	前往 go to			双 shuāng	一双 pair	
量 liàng	测量 measure			服 fú	服务 service	
早 zǎo	早 early			击 jī	攻击 attack	
结 jié	结束 end			武 wǔ	武术 martial arts	
怕 pà	害怕 fear			哪 nǎ	哪里 where	
流 liú	流水 water flow			数 shù	数字 number	
突 tū	突然 sudden			站 zhàn	站立 stand	
坐 zuò	坐下 sit down			奇 qí	奇怪 odd	
斯 sī	斯坦福 Stanford, sounds like si			房 fáng	房间 room	
				管 guǎn	管道 tube	
音 yīn	声音 sound			灵 líng	灵魂 spirit	
紧 jǐn	紧张 nervous			刻 kè	一刻 moment	
指 zhǐ	手指 finger			题 tí	问题 question	
拉 lā	拉开 pull apart			衣 yī	衣服 clothes	
杀 shā	杀死 kill			周 zhōu	一周 week	
半 bàn	一半 half			静 jìng	安静 quite	
记 jì	记住 remember			伤 shāng	受伤 injured	
且 qiě	而且 and			百 bǎi	一百 hundred	
利 lì	利益 benefit			拿 ná	拿来 bring it	
合 hé	合并 combine			妈 mā	妈妈 Mom	
倒 dào	倒推 reverse			办 bàn	办理 deal with	
书 shū	书本 book			星 xīng	星星 star	
度 dù	温度 temperature			化 huà	变化 change	
微 wēi	微小 micro			功 gōng	成功 achievement	
步 bù	脚步 step			绝 jué	绝对 absolute	
教 jiāo	教导 teach			系 xì	系统 system	
喜 xǐ	喜悦 joy			般 bān	一般 general	
越 yuè	越过 transit			必 bì	必须 must	
影 yǐng	影子 shadow			业 yè	业务 business	
谁 shéi	谁 who			尔 ěr	诺贝尔 Nobel, sounds like er	
冷 lěng	寒冷 cold					
深 shēn	深 deep			件 jiàn	一件 a piece	
告 gào	告诉 notice			血 xuè	血液 blood	
落 luò	落下 fall			代 dài	一代 a generation	

精 jīng	精美 fine			欢 huān	欢乐 happy
弟 dì	弟弟 little brother			字 zì	字 word
终 zhōng	终结 end			晚 wǎn	晚上 night
近 jìn	附近 nearby			民 mín	人民 people
条 tiáo	条件 condition			帮 bāng	帮助 help
青 qīng	青年 youth			切 qiè	切割 cut
界 jiè	世界 world			即 jí	立即 immediate
司 sī	公司 company				
整 zhěng	整个 whole				

401–500

忙 máng	忙碌 busy	刘 liú	刘 Liu
交 jiāo	交通 transportation	极 jí	极限 limit
或 huò	或者 or	识 shí	知识 knowledge
暗 àn	黑暗 dark	备 bèi	准备 prepare
夫 fū	丈夫 husband	慢 màn	缓慢 slow
员 yuán	成员 member	雪 xuě	雪 snow
根 gēn	树根 root	苦 kǔ	吃苦 suffering
石 shí	石头 stone	若 Ruò	倘若 if
哈 hā	撒哈拉 Sahara, sounds like ha	领 lǐng	领导 lead
夜 yè	夜晚 night	收 shōu	接收 receive
父 fù	父亲 father	底 dǐ	底部 bottom
制 zhì	控制 control	尽 jǐn	尽头 end
友 yǒu	朋友 friend	准 zhǔn	准确 accurate
阿 ā	阿拉伯 Arab, sounds like Ah	华 huá	华人 Chinese
息 xī	休息 rest	答 dá	回答 answer
冲 chōng	冲击 impact	众 zhòng	众人 people
酒 jiǔ	酒 wine	千 qiān	千 thousand
保 bǎo	保护 protect	消 xiāo	消费 consume
片 piàn	影片 film	视 shì	视力 vision
形 xíng	形状 shape	罗 luó	罗列 list
阵 Zhèn	阵线 front	敢 gǎn	敢于 dare
南 nán	南方 south	留 liú	留下 stay
决 jué	决定 decide	克 kè	克服 overcome
请 qǐng	请 please	乐 lè	快乐 happy
各 gè	各位 everyone	够 gòu	足够 enough
报 bào	报告 report	跑 pǎo	跑步 run
兴 xìng	兴奋 excite	显 xiǎn	显示 show
阳 yáng	太阳 sun	嘴 Zuǐ	嘴巴 mouth
急 jí	紧急 urgent	官 guān	官员 official
语 yǔ	言语 words	断 duàn	断绝 break off
令 lìng	命令 order	未 wèi	未来 future
错 cuò	错误 wrong	势 shì	势力 power
及 jí	及其 and	句 jù	句子 sentence
		求 qiú	寻求 seek
		计 jì	计划 plan

论 lùn	讨论 discuss	玉 yù	玉 jade
达 dá	到达 reach	沉 chén	沉底 sink
则 zé	则 then	北 běi	北方 north
害 hài	害怕 afraid	格 gé	格子 grid
八 bā	八 eight	停 tíng	停止 stop
单 dān	单个 single	陈 chén	陈述 statement
久 jiǔ	长 long	市 shì	城市 city
脚 jiǎo	脚 foot	朝 cháo	朝向 toward
德 dé	道德 morality	喝 hē	喝水 drink
元 yuán	元 currency unit yuan	族 zú	民族 nationality
脑 nǎo	脑 brain	江 jiāng	江河 river
楚 chǔ	清楚 clear	团 tuán	团体 group
雨 Yǔ	下雨 rain	母 mǔ	母亲 mother
睛 jīng	眼睛 eye	章 zhāng	章程 chapter
响 xiǎng	响声 sound	装 zhuāng	装扮 dress up
刀 dāo	刀 knife		
确 què	确实 sure		

501–600

亮 liàng	明亮 bright	痛 tòng	疼痛 pain
客 kè	客人 guest	梦 mèng	梦想 dream
照 zhào	照片 photo	呼 hū	呼叫 call
乱 luàn	混乱 chaos	摇 yáo	摇晃 shake
易 yì	容易 easy	期 qī	期间 period
足 zú	足 foot	英 yīng	英语 English
依 yī	依靠 depend	低 dī	低 low
黄 huáng	黄色 yellow	帝 dì	皇帝 emperor
修 xiū	修理 repair	兄 xiōng	兄弟 brother
破 pò	破碎 broken	背 bèi	背负 carry
台 tái	台湾 Taiwan	持 chí	坚持 persist
球 qiú	球 ball	爷 yé	爷爷 grandfather
呀 ya	天呀 Oh my god	皇 huáng	皇帝 emperor
院 yuàn	院子 court	七 qī	七 seven
送 sòng	送 send	六 liù	六 six
包 bāo	包裹 package	穿 chuān	穿过 cross
义 yì	义气 loyalty	杨 yáng	杨柳 willow
诉 sù	告诉 tell	政 zhèng	政府 government
攻 gōng	攻击 attack	运 yùn	运动 sports
丝 sī	丝绸 silk	居 jū	居住 reside
围 wéi	包围 surround	叶 yè	树叶 leaves
玩 wán	玩耍 play	热 rè	热 hot
待 dài	等待 wait	校 xiào	学校 school
复 fù	恢复 recover	谢 xiè	谢谢 thank
况 kuàng	情况 condition	曾 céng	曾经 once
楼 lóu	楼房 building	古 gǔ	古代 ancient
丽 lì	美丽 beautiful	细 xì	细小 small

产 chǎn	产品 product	程 chéng	工程 enginnering
睡 shuì	睡觉 sleep	首 shǒu	首先 first
希 xī	希望 hope	观 guān	观点 view
速 sù	速度 speed	朋 péng	朋友 friends
室 shì	室 room	务 wù	任务 duty
旁 páng	旁边 beside	掉 diào	掉下 drop
另 lìng	另外 another	赶 gǎn	赶上 catch up
怀 huái	关怀 care	忽 hū	忽然 suddenly
露 lù	露水 dew	注 zhù	注意 notice
异 yì	异常 abnormal	术 shù	技术 technology
写 xiě	书写 write	甚 shèn	甚至 even
鬼 guǐ	鬼魂 ghost	差 chà	差距 gap
娘 niáng	娘 mother	呵 hē	笑呵呵 laugh haha
取 qǔ	取得 obtain	展 zhǎn	展览 exhibit
式 shì	式样 style	争 zhēng	争论 debate
除 chú	除去 remove	品 pǐn	产品 product
级 jí	年级 grade	兰 lán	兰花 orchid
考 kǎo	考试 examination	宝 bǎo	宝贝 treasured object
建 jiàn	建筑 construct	香 xiāng	香味 fragrance
愿 yuàn	愿 wish	斗 dòu	斗争 fight
招 zhāo	招待 entertain	故 gù	故事 story
饭 fàn	米饭 rice	雷 léi	打雷 thunder
布 bù	布匹 cloth		
续 xù	继续 continue		

www.ingramcontent.com/pod-product-compliance
Lightning Source LLC
Chambersburg PA
CBHW071906020426
42331CB00010B/2697